CHILD SUPPORT ENFORCEMENT PROGRAM

ELEMENTS, FINANCIAL ISSUES, AND INCENTIVE PAYMENT POLICIES

CHILDREN'S ISSUES, LAWS AND PROGRAMS

Additional books in this series can be found on Nova's website under the Series tab.

Additional E-books in this series can be found on Nova's website under the E-book tab.

SOCIAL ISSUES, JUSTICE AND STATUS

Additional books in this series can be found on Nova's website under the Series tab.

Additional E-books in this series can be found on Nova's website under the E-book tab.

CHILDREN'S ISSUES, LAWS AND PROGRAMS

CHILD SUPPORT ENFORCEMENT PROGRAM

ELEMENTS, FINANCIAL ISSUES, AND INCENTIVE PAYMENT POLICIES

PASCAL CHOLLET
EDITOR

nova publishers
New York

For permission to use material from this book please contact us:
Telephone 631-231-7269; Fax 631-231-8175
Web Site: http://www.novapublishers.com

NOTICE TO THE READER

The Publisher has taken reasonable care in the preparation of this book, but makes no expressed or implied warranty of any kind and assumes no responsibility for any errors or omissions. No liability is assumed for incidental or consequential damages in connection with or arising out of information contained in this book. The Publisher shall not be liable for any special, consequential, or exemplary damages resulting, in whole or in part, from the readers' use of, or reliance upon, this material. Any parts of this book based on government reports are so indicated and copyright is claimed for those parts to the extent applicable to compilations of such works.

Independent verification should be sought for any data, advice or recommendations contained in this book. In addition, no responsibility is assumed by the publisher for any injury and/or damage to persons or property arising from any methods, products, instructions, ideas or otherwise contained in this publication.

This publication is designed to provide accurate and authoritative information with regard to the subject matter covered herein. It is sold with the clear understanding that the Publisher is not engaged in rendering legal or any other professional services. If legal or any other expert assistance is required, the services of a competent person should be sought. FROM A DECLARATION OF PARTICIPANTS JOINTLY ADOPTED BY A COMMITTEE OF THE AMERICAN BAR ASSOCIATION AND A COMMITTEE OF PUBLISHERS.

Additional color graphics may be available in the e-book version of this book.

Library of Congress Cataloging-in-Publication Data

ISBN: 978-1-62808-384-2

Published by Nova Science Publishers, Inc. † *New York*

CONTENTS

PREFACE

The Child Support Enforcement (CSE) program was enacted in 1975 as a federal-state program (Title IV-D of the Social Security Act) to help strengthen families by securing financial support for children from their noncustodial parent on a consistent and continuing basis and by helping some families to remain self-sufficient and off public assistance by providing the requisite CSE services. Over the years, CSE has evolved into a multifaceted program. While cost-recovery still remains an important function of the program, its other aspects include service delivery and promotion of self-sufficiency and parental responsibility. In FY2011, the CSE program collected $27.3 billion in child support payments and served nearly 15.8 million child support cases. However, the program still collects only 62% of current child support obligations for which it has responsibility and collects payments for only 57% of its caseload. This book examines the background, financial issues and incentive payment policies for the Child Support Enforcement Program.

Chapter 1 - The CSE program, Part D of Title IV of the Social Security Act, was enacted in January 1975 (P.L. 93-647). The CSE program is administered by the Office of Child Support Enforcement (OCSE) in the Department of Health and Human Services (HHS), and funded by general revenues. All 50 states, the District of Columbia, Guam, Puerto Rico, and the Virgin Islands operate CSE programs and are entitled to federal matching funds.[1] Families receiving Temporary Assistance for Needy Families (TANF) benefits (Title IV-A of the Social Security Act), foster care payments, or Medicaid coverage automatically qualify for CSE services free of charge. Collections on behalf of families receiving cash TANF block grant benefits are used, in part, to reimburse state and federal governments for TANF payments made to the family. Other families must apply for CSE services, and states must charge an application fee that cannot exceed $25.[2] Child support collected on behalf of nonwelfare families goes to the family, usually through the state disbursement unit.

Between FY1978 and FY2011, child support payments collected by CSE agencies increased from $1 billion in FY1978 to $27.3 billion in FY2011, and the number of children whose paternity was established or acknowledged increased from 111,000 to 1.687 million. However, the program still collects only 20% of child support obligations for which it has responsibility if arrearage payments are taken into account (otherwise, 62%)[3] and collects payments for only 57% of its caseload. OCSE data indicate that in FY2011, paternity had been established or acknowledged for 94% of the 11.2 million children on the CSE caseload without legally identified fathers.[4] The CSE program is estimated to handle 50%-60% of all child support cases; the remaining cases are handled by private attorneys, collection agencies, or through mutual agreements between the parents.

Chapter 2 – The Deficit Reduction Act of 2005 (P.L. 109-171) made changes to the Child Support Enforcement (CSE) program that will result in less federal financial support to state CSE programs. The CSE program serves families that are recipients of the Temporary Assistance for Needy Families (TANF) program and non-recipient families. It provides seven major services: parent location, paternity establishment, establishment of child support orders, review and modification of support orders, collection of child support payments, distribution of support payments, and establishment and enforcement of medical child support orders. In FY2010, the CSE system handled 15.9 million cases, of which 86% (13.7 million) were non-TANF cases. In FY2010, the CSE program expenditures amounted to nearly $5.8 billion and the program collected $4.88 in child support payments (from noncustodial parents) for every dollar spent on the program.

The federal government bears the majority of CSE program expenditures and provides incentive payments to the states for success in meeting CSE goals. Most child support collections for TANF families are kept by the federal government and states to reimburse themselves for the cost of providing TANF cash payments to those families. Collections for non-TANF families generally are paid to the families (via the state CSE disbursement unit).

Some policymakers are concerned that the federal government's role in financing CSE is too high, and contend that the states should pay a greater share of the program's costs. Comparing CSE expenditures with the income generated by retained collections for TANF families, the federal government has lost money each year since 1979 (the FY2009 "loss" to the federal government was $2.9 billion). Although in the past the income generated by the CSE program for states (in the aggregate) exceeded their expenses, this no longer holds true (the FY2009 "loss" to states was $718 million). The increasing federal "losses" on the CSE program and the switch from "gain" to "loss" for the state governments is in part attributable to the decline in the TANF caseload.

An alternative analysis views retained child support collections as reimbursement for a portion of cash welfare expenditures for families with children, rather than as "income" to the state. The share of AFDC/TANF cash expenditures reimbursed by child support collections grew consistently during the period from FY1994 through FY2002, when CSE collections for welfare families remained relatively stable, while cash welfare payments decreased dramatically, from $22.7 billion in FY1994 to $9.4 billion in FY2002. Between FY2002 and FY2010, AFDC/TANF cash expenditures fluctuated up and down. In FY1994, retained child support collections for welfare families as a percentage of total cash welfare expenditures was 11%; by FY2010, it was about 18% (after reaching a high point of nearly 31% in FY2002).

The change in the composition of the CSE caseload, together with changes made pursuant to P.L. 109-171, are expected to result in state CSE programs having to compete with all other state interests in obtaining funds from the general treasury or county treasuries. This is a dramatic departure from the past, when the CSE program was unique among social welfare programs in that it added money to state treasuries.

Chapter 3 – The Child Support Enforcement (CSE) program, enacted in 1975, to help strengthen families by securing financial support from noncustodial parents, is funded with both state and federal dollars. The federal government bears the majority of CSE program expenditures and provides incentive payments to the states (which include Washington, DC, and the territories of Guam, Puerto Rico, and the Virgin Islands) for success in meeting CSE program goals. In FY2011, total CSE program expenditures amounted to $5.7 billion. The aggregate incentive payment amount to states was $513 million in FY2011.

P.L. 105-200, the Child Support Performance and Incentive Act of 1998, established a revised incentive payment system that provides incentive payments to states based on a percentage of the state's CSE collections and incorporates five performance measures related to establishment of paternity and child support orders, collections of current and past-due support payments, and cost-effectiveness. P.L. 105-200 set specific annual caps on total federal incentive payments and required states to reinvest incentive payments back into the CSE program. The exact amount of a state's incentive payment depends on its level of performance (or the rate of improvement over the previous year) when compared with other states. In addition, states are required to meet data quality standards. If states do not meet specified performance measures and data quality standards, they face federal financial penalties.

P.L. 109-171 (the Deficit Reduction Act of 2005) prohibited federal matching (effective October 1, 2007, i.e., FY2008) of state expenditure of federal CSE incentive payments. However, in 2009 P.L. 111-5 (the American Recovery and Reinvestment Act of 2009) required the Department of Health and Human Services (HHS) to temporarily provide federal matching funds (in FY2009 and FY2010) on CSE incentive payments that states reinvested back into the CSE program. Thus (since FY2011), CSE incentive payments that are received by states and reinvested in the CSE program are no longer eligible for federal reimbursement. The FY2008 repeal of federal reimbursement for incentive payments reinvested in the CSE program garnered much concern over its fiscal impact on the states and renewed interest in the incentive payment system per se.

A comparison of FY2002 incentive payment performance score data to FY2011 performance score data shows that CSE program performance has improved with respect to all five performance measures. Although CSE incentive payments were awarded to all 54 jurisdictions in FY2002, FY2005, FY2010, and FY2011 (the years covered in this report), some jurisdictions performed poorly on one or more of the five performance measures. Even so, on the basis of the unaudited FY2011 performance incentive scores of the 54 jurisdictions, 53 jurisdictions received an incentive for all five performance measures, and 1 jurisdiction (the Virgin Islands) received an incentive for four performance measures.

Despite a general consensus that the CSE program is doing well, questions still arise about whether the program is effectively meeting its mission and concerns exist over whether the program will be able to meet future expectations. Several factors may cause a state not to receive an incentive payment that is commensurate with its relative performance on individual measures. These factors include static or declining CSE collections; sliding scale performance scores that financially benefit states at the upper end (but not the top) of the artificial threshold and financially disadvantaged states at the lower end of the artificial threshold; a limited number of performance indicators that do not encompass all of the components critical to a successful

CSE program; and a statutory maximum on the aggregate amount of incentive payments that can be paid to states. These factors are discussed in the context of the following policy questions: (1) Does the CSE incentive payment system reward good performance? (2) Should incentive payments be based on additional performance indicators? (3) Should Temporary Assistance for Needy Families (TANF) funds be reduced because of poor CSE performance? (4) Why aren't the incentives and penalties consistent for the paternity establishment performance measure? (5) Should incentive payments be based on individual state performance rather than aggregate state performance? and (6) Will the elimination of the federal match of incentive payments adversely affect CSE programs?

Chapter 4 – P.L. 109-171, the Deficit Reduction Act of 2005, required states to impose a $25 annual user fee for Child Support Enforcement (CSE) services provided to families with no connection to the welfare system. The user fee is to be assessed if the state CSE agency collects at least $500 in child support payments on behalf of the family in a given fiscal year. The law gives the states four options on how to obtain the user fee. According to an August 2012 survey of the 54 jurisdictions with CSE programs, 18 jurisdictions pay the fee with state funds, 4 jurisdictions get the fee from the noncustodial parent, 1 jurisdiction imposes the user fee directly on the custodial parent, and 31 jurisdictions impose the fee indirectly on the custodial parent by retaining the fee from the family's child support payment (after $500 per year has been collected on behalf of the family).

In: Child Support Enforcement Program   ISBN: 978-1-62808-384-2
Editor: Pascal Chollet   © 2013 Nova Science Publishers, Inc.

Chapter 1

CHILD SUPPORT ENFORCEMENT: PROGRAM BASICS[*]

Carmen Solomon-Fears

SUMMARY

The Child Support Enforcement (CSE) program was enacted in 1975 as a federal-state program (Title IV-D of the Social Security Act) to help strengthen families by securing financial support for children from their noncustodial parent on a consistent and continuing basis and by helping some families to remain self-sufficient and off public assistance by providing the requisite CSE services. Over the years, CSE has evolved into a multifaceted program. While cost-recovery still remains an important function of the program, its other aspects include service delivery and promotion of self-sufficiency and parental responsibility. In FY2011, the CSE program collected $27.3 billion in child support payments and served nearly 15.8 million child support cases. However, the program still collects only 62% of current child support obligations for which it has responsibility and collects payments for only 57% of its caseload.

---

[*] This is an edited, reformatted and augmented version of a Congressional Research Service publication, CRS Report for Congress RS22380, prepared for Members and Committees of Congress, from www.crs.gov, dated November 5, 2012.

BACKGROUND

The CSE program, Part D of Title IV of the Social Security Act, was enacted in January 1975 (P.L. 93-647). The CSE program is administered by the Office of Child Support Enforcement (OCSE) in the Department of Health and Human Services (HHS), and funded by general revenues. All 50 states, the District of Columbia, Guam, Puerto Rico, and the Virgin Islands operate CSE programs and are entitled to federal matching funds.[1] Families receiving Temporary Assistance for Needy Families (TANF) benefits (Title IV-A of the Social Security Act), foster care payments, or Medicaid coverage automatically qualify for CSE services free of charge. Collections on behalf of families receiving cash TANF block grant benefits are used, in part, to reimburse state and federal governments for TANF payments made to the family. Other families must apply for CSE services, and states must charge an application fee that cannot exceed $25.[2] Child support collected on behalf of nonwelfare families goes to the family, usually through the state disbursement unit.

Between FY1978 and FY2011, child support payments collected by CSE agencies increased from $1 billion in FY1978 to $27.3 billion in FY2011, and the number of children whose paternity was established or acknowledged increased from 111,000 to 1.687 million. However, the program still collects only 20% of child support obligations for which it has responsibility if arrearage payments are taken into account (otherwise, 62%)[3] and collects payments for only 57% of its caseload. OCSE data indicate that in FY2011, paternity had been established or acknowledged for 94% of the 11.2 million children on the CSE caseload without legally identified fathers.[4] The CSE program is estimated to handle 50%-60% of all child support cases; the remaining cases are handled by private attorneys, collection agencies, or through mutual agreements between the parents.

PROGRAM ELEMENTS

The CSE program provides seven major services on behalf of children: (1) parent location, (2) paternity establishment, (3) establishment of child support orders, (4) review and modification of child support orders, (5) collection of child support payments, (6) distribution of child support payments, and (7) establishment and enforcement of medical support.[5]

Table 1. Child Support Data—FY2011 (Preliminary)

Total CSE caseload	Total, 15.8 million; TANF, 2.0 million; former-TANF, 6.8 million; never-TANF, 7.0 million
Total CSE collections	Total, $27.297 billion; TANF families, $1.010 billion; former-TANF, $8.930 billion; never-TANF, $11.822 billion (plus $5.535 billion on behalf of Medicaid-only families)
Payments to families	Total, $25.1 billion; TANF, $167 million; former-TANF, $7.9 billion; never-TANF, $11.7 billion (plus $5.4 billion on behalf of Medicaid-only families)
Federal share of TANF collections	$923 million
State share of TANF collections	$719 million
Medical support payments	$365 million
Total CSE expenditures	$5.661 billion; federal share, $3.477 billion, state share, $2.184 billion
Incentive payments to states (estimated)	$465 million
Paternities established and acknowledged	1,686,980
Support orders established	1,248,046 (includes only new orders; excludes modifications)
Collections made	For 9,005,857 total families; TANF families, 691,827; former-TANF families, 3,855,684; never-TANF families, 4,458,346

Source: Table prepared by the Congressional Research Service, based on data from the Office of Child Support Enforcement, Department of Health and Human Services.

Note: Some totals are imprecise because of rounding.

Locating Absent Parents

To improve the CSE agency's ability to locate absent parents, states are required to have automated registries of child support orders that contain records of each case in which CSE services are being provided and all new or modified child support orders. The state registry includes a record of the support owed under the order, arrearages, interest or late penalty charges, amounts collected, amounts distributed, the child's date of birth, and any liens imposed; and also includes standardized information on both parents, such as name, Social Security number, date of birth, and case identification number.

States also must establish an automated directory of new hires containing information from employers, including federal, state, and local governments and labor organizations, for each newly hired employee, that includes the name, address, and Social Security number of the employee and the employer's name, address, and tax identification number. This information generally is supplied to the state new hires directory within 20 days after the employee is hired. Moreover, federal law required the establishment of a federal case registry of child support orders and a national directory of new hires.[6] The federal directories consist of information from the state directories and federal agencies (located in the Federal Parent Locator Service, or FPLS).

Federal law allows all states to link up to an array of databases, and permits the FPLS to be used for the purpose of establishing parentage; establishing, setting the amount of, modifying, or enforcing child support obligations; and enforcing child custody or visitation orders.[7] Federal law requires that a designated state agency, directly or by contract, conduct automated comparisons of the Social Security numbers reported by employers to the state directory of new hires and the Social Security numbers of CSE cases that appear in the records of the state registry of child support orders. Federal law requires the HHS Secretary to conduct similar comparisons of the federal directories.[8] Automation is critical to the operation and success of the CSE program.[9]

Paternity Establishment

Legally identifying the father is a prerequisite for obtaining a child support order. Federal law requires TANF applicants and recipients to cooperate in establishing paternity or obtaining support payments. Moreover, a penalty for noncooperation exists. If it is determined that an individual is not cooperating and the individual does not qualify for any good cause or other exception, then the state must reduce the family's TANF benefit by at least 25% and may eliminate it entirely. Federal law also (1) requires that paternity be established for 90% of the CSE cases needing such a determination, (2) requires a simple civil process for establishing paternity, (3) requires an affidavit to be completed by men voluntarily acknowledging paternity and entitles the affidavit to full faith and credit in any state, (4) stipulates that a signed acknowledgment of paternity be considered a legal finding of paternity unless it is rescinded within 60 days, and thereafter may be challenged in court only on the basis of fraud, duress, or material mistake of fact, (5) provides that no judicial or administrative action is needed to ratify an acknowledgment that is not challenged, and (6) requires all parties to submit to genetic testing in contested paternity cases.

Establishment of Child Support Orders

A child support order legally obligates noncustodial parents to provide financial support for their children and stipulates the amount of the obligation and how it is to be paid. It is usually established at the time of divorce or when an unmarried couple dissolves their relationship or when a welfare case is initiated. P.L. 100-485 required states to use their state-established guidelines in establishing child support orders. States decide child support amounts based on the noncustodial parent's income or based on both parents' income; other factors include the age of child, whether a stepparent is in the home, whether the child is disabled, and the number of siblings.

Review and Modification of Support Orders

Without periodic modifications, child support obligations can become inadequate or inequitable. Under current law, states generally must review child support orders every three years to determine if the order should be adjusted to reflect the parent's financial circumstances.[10]

Enforcement

Collection methods used by state CSE agencies include income withholding,[11] intercept of federal and state income tax refunds, intercept of unemployment compensation, liens against property, reporting child support obligations to credit bureaus, intercept of lottery winnings, sending insurance settlement information to CSE agencies, authority to withhold or suspend driver's licenses, professional licenses, and recreational and sporting licenses of persons who owe past-due support, and authority to seize assets of debtor parents held by public or private retirement funds and financial institutions. Moreover, federal law authorizes the Secretary of State to deny, revoke, or restrict passports of debtor parents. All jurisdictions also have civil or criminal contempt-of-court procedures and criminal nonsupport laws. In addition, federal criminal penalties may be imposed in certain cases. Federal law also requires states to enact and implement the Uniform Interstate Family Support Act (UIFSA), and expand full faith and credit procedures. Federal law also provides for international enforcement of child support.[12]

Financing[13]

The federal government reimburses each state 66% of the cost of operating its CSE program.[14] In addition, the federal government pays states an incentive payment to encourage them to operate effective programs.[15] Federal law requires states to reinvest CSE incentive payments back into the CSE program or related activities.[16]

Collection and Disbursement

All states are required to have a centralized automated state collection and disbursement unit to which child support payments are paid and from which they are distributed. Federal law generally requires employers to remit to the state disbursement unit (SDU) income withheld within seven business days after the employee's payday. Further, the SDU is required to send child support payments to custodial parents within two business days of receipt of such payments.

Distribution of Support

Distribution rules determine which claim is paid first when a child support collection occurs. The order of payment of the child support collection is important because in many cases arrearages are never fully paid. While the family receives TANF cash benefits, the states and federal government retain any current support and any assigned arrearages[17] collected up to the cumulative amount of TANF benefits paid to the family. While states may pay their share of collections to the family, they must pay the federal government the federal government's share of child support collections collected on behalf of TANF families. This means that the state, and not the federal government, bears the entire cost of any child support passed through to families (and disregarded by the state in determining the family's TANF cash benefit).[18]

Based on June 2009 data, 19 states and the District of Columbia have a CSE pass-through and disregard policy and 31 states do not.[19]

States must distribute to former TANF families the following child support collections first before the state and the federal government are reimbursed (the "family-first" policy): (1) all current child support, (2) any child support arrearages that accrue after the family leaves TANF (these arrearages are called never-assigned arrearages), plus (3) any arrearages that accrued before the family began receiving TANF benefits. An exception to this rule occurs when child support arrearages are collected via the federal income tax refund offset program—those collections are divided between the state and federal government.[20] (Any child support arrearages that accrue during the time the family is on TANF belong to the state and federal government.)

VISITATION GRANTS AND RESPONSIBLE FATHERHOOD PROGRAMS

Historically, Congress has agreed that visitation and child support should be legally separate issues, and that only child support should be under the purview of the CSE program. Both federal and state policymakers have maintained that denial of visitation rights should be treated separately, and should not be considered a reason for stopping child support payments. However, in recognition of the negative long-term consequences for children associated with the absence of their father, P.L. 104-193 provided an annual entitlement of $10 million from the federal CSE budget account for grants to states for access and visitation programs, including mediation, counseling, education, and supervised visitation.

P.L. 109-171 provided $50 million per year for five years (FY2006-FY2010) in competitive grants (under Title IV-A of the Social Security Act) for responsible fatherhood programs to states, territories, Indian tribes and tribal organizations, and public and nonprofit organizations, including religious organizations.

P.L. 111-291 (enacted December 8, 2010) extended funding for the Title IV-A Healthy Marriage and Responsible Fatherhood grants through FY2011. For FY2011, P.L. 111-291 appropriated $75 million for awarding funds for healthy marriage promotion activities and $75 million for awarding funds for activities promoting responsible fatherhood. The result is that the Title IV-A

Healthy Marriage and Responsible Fatherhood grants, which were funded at
$150 million annually from FY2006 through FY2010, were funded for an
additional year (FY2011) on an equal basis.

Pursuant to P.L. 112-78 (enacted December 23, 2011), the Healthy
Marriage and Responsible Fatherhood grant programs were extended at their
FY2011 funding level (on a pro rata basis) through February 29, 2012.
Pursuant to P.L. 112-96 (enacted February 22, 2012), the Healthy Marriage
and Responsible Fatherhood grant programs were extended (at their FY2011
funding level) through the end of FY2012 (on a pro rata basis). (For more
information on responsible fatherhood programs, see CRS Report RL31025,
Fatherhood Initiatives: Connecting Fathers to Their Children, by Carmen
Solomon-Fears.)

End Notes

[1] States were historically required to provide CSE services to Indian tribes and tribal
organizations as part of their CSE caseloads. In contrast to the federal matching rate of 66%
for CSE programs run by the states or territories, pursuant to the 1996 welfare reform law
(P.L. 104-193), the CSE program provides direct federal funding equal to 100% of
approved and allowable CSE expenditures during the start-up period, provides 90% federal
funding for approved CSE programs operated by tribes or tribal organizations during the
first three years of full program operation, and provides 80% federal funding thereafter. In
FY2011, 42 Indian tribes or tribal organizations operated comprehensive tribal CSE
programs and as of August 2012, 13 Indian tribes or tribal organizations operated start-up
tribal CSE programs. (For additional information, see CRS Report R41204, Child Support
Enforcement: Tribal Programs, by Carmen Solomon-Fears.)

[2] P.L. 109-171, effective October 1, 2006, requires families who have never been on TANF to
pay a $25 annual user fee when child support enforcement efforts on their behalf are
successful (i.e., at least $500 annually is collected on their behalf). For more information on
the CSE annual user fee, see CRS Report RS22735, Spending by Employers on Health
Insurance: A Data Brief, by Jennifer Jenson.

[3] In FY2011, $144.6 billion in child support obligations ($33.3 billion in current support and
$111.3 billion in past-due support) was owed to families receiving CSE services, but only
$28.5 billion was paid ($20.8 billion current, $7.7 billion past-due).

[4] For more information regarding FY2011 data on the CSE program, see http://www.acf.hhs.
gov/programs/css/ resource/fy2011-preliminary-report#tables.

[5] A noncustodial parent may be ordered to provide health insurance if available through his or her
employer, pay for private health insurance premiums, or reimburse the custodial parent for
all or a portion of the costs of health insurance obtained by the custodial parent. Federal law
requires every child support order to include a provision for health care coverage. The CSE
program is required to pursue private health care coverage when such coverage is available
through a noncustodial parent's employer at a reasonable cost. P.L. 109-171 required that
medical support for a child be provided by either or both parents and that it must be

enforced. It authorizes the state CSE agency to enforce medical support against a custodial parent whenever health care coverage is available to the custodial parent at reasonable cost. Moreover, it stipulates that medical support may include health care coverage (including payment of costs of premiums, co-payments, and deductibles) and payment of medical expenses for a child.

[6] Within three business days after receipt of new hire information from the employer, the state directory of new hires is required to furnish the information to the national directory of new hires. (For additional information, see CRS Report RS22889, The National Directory of New Hires, by Carmen Solomon-Fears.)

[7] P.L. 104-193 permitted both custodial and certain noncustodial parents to obtain information from the FPLS. P.L. 105-33, however, prohibited FPLS information from being disclosed to noncustodial parents in cases where there is evidence of domestic violence or child abuse, and the local court determines that disclosure may result in harm to the custodial parent or child.

[8] When a match occurs, the state directory of new hires is required to report to the state CSE agency the name, address, and Social Security number of the employee, and the employer's name, address, and identification number. Within two business days, the CSE agency then instructs appropriate employers to withhold child support obligations from the employee's paycheck, unless the employee's income is not subject to income withholding.

[9] Federal law requires suspension of all federal CSE funding to the state when its CSE plan, after appeal, is disapproved. Moreover, states without approved CSE plans could lose funding for the TANF block grant. P.L. 105-200 imposed substantially smaller financial penalties on states that failed to meet the automated data systems requirements. The HHS Secretary is required to reduce the amount the state would otherwise have received in federal CSE funding by the penalty amount for the fiscal year in question. The penalty amount percentage is 4% in the case of the first year of noncompliance (FY1998); 8% in the second year (FY1999); 16% in the third year (FY2000); 25% in the fourth year (FY2001); and 30% in the fifth or any subsequent year.

[10] If a noncustodial parent cannot pay his or her child support payments because of unemployment, imprisonment, and so forth, then the noncustodial parent should immediately contact the court in order to have the child support order modified. Pursuant to federal law (section 466(a)(9) of the Social Security Act), the court will not be able to retroactively reduce the back payments (i.e., arrearages) that a noncustodial parent owes.

[11] There are three exceptions to the immediate income withholding rule: (1) if one of the parties demonstrates, and the court (or administrative process) finds that there is good cause not to require immediate withholding, (2) if both parties agree in writing to an alternative arrangement, or (3) at the HHS Secretary's discretion, if a state can demonstrate that the rule will not increase the effectiveness or efficiency of the state's CSE program.

[12] The CSE program has reciprocating agreements regarding the enforcement of child support with 15 countries: Australia, Canada, Czech Republic, El Salvador, Finland, Hungary, Ireland, Israel, Netherlands, Norway, Poland, Portugal, Slovak Republic, Switzerland, and the United Kingdom of Great Britain and Northern Ireland.

[13] For additional information on the financing of the CSE program, see CRS Report RL33422, Analysis of Federal-State Financing of the Child Support Enforcement Program, by Carmen Solomon-Fears.

[14] P.L. 109-171 stipulated that the 90% federal matching rate for laboratory costs associated with paternity establishment would be reduced to 66% beginning October 1, 2006.

[15] The CSE incentive payment—which is based in part on five performance measures related to establishment of paternity and child support orders, collection of current and past-due child support payments, and cost-effectiveness— was statutorily set by P.L. 105-200. In the aggregate, incentive payments to states may not exceed $458 million for FY2006, $471 million for FY2007, and $483 million for FY2008 (to be increased for inflation in years thereafter). Aggregate incentive payments to states are capped at $513 million for FY2011 and estimated to amount to $465 million. For additional information on CSE incentive payments, see CRS Report RL34203, Child Support Enforcement Program Incentive Payments: Background and Policy Issues, by Carmen Solomon-Fears.

[16] P.L. 109-171, effective October 1, 2007, prohibited federal matching of state expenditure of federal CSE incentive payments. However, P.L. 111-5 required HHS to temporarily provide federal matching funds (in FY2009 and FY2010) on CSE incentive payments that states reinvest back into the CSE program. Thus, CSE incentive payments that are received by states and reinvested in the CSE program are no longer eligible for federal reimbursement.

[17] The child support assignment covers any child support that accrues while the family receives cash TANF benefits, as well as any child support that accrued before the family started receiving TANF benefits. Pursuant to P.L. 109-171 (effective October 1, 2009, or at state option, October 1, 2008), the assignment only covers child support that accrues while the family receives TANF.

[18] P.L. 109-171 helps states pay for the cost of their CSE pass-through and disregard policies by requiring the federal government to share in the costs of the entire amount (up to $100 per month for one child; up to $200 per month for two or more children) of child support collections passed through and disregarded by states (effective October 1, 2008).

[19] Michelle Vinson and Vicki Turetsky, "State Child Support Pass-Through Policies," Center for Law and Social Policy, June 12, 2009.

[20] P.L. 109-171 gives states the option of distributing to former TANF families the full amount of child support collected on their behalf (i.e., both current support and all child support arrearages—including arrearages collected through the federal income tax refund offset program). This provision took effect on October 1, 2009, or October 1, 2008, at state option.

In: Child Support Enforcement Program   ISBN: 978-1-62808-384-2
Editor: Pascal Chollet   © 2013 Nova Science Publishers, Inc.

Chapter 2

ANALYSIS OF FEDERAL-STATE FINANCING OF THE CHILD SUPPORT ENFORCEMENT PROGRAM*

Carmen Solomon-Fears

SUMMARY

The Deficit Reduction Act of 2005 (P.L. 109-171) made changes to the Child Support Enforcement (CSE) program that will result in less federal financial support to state CSE programs. The CSE program serves families that are recipients of the Temporary Assistance for Needy Families (TANF) program and non-recipient families. It provides seven major services: parent location, paternity establishment, establishment of child support orders, review and modification of support orders, collection of child support payments, distribution of support payments, and establishment and enforcement of medical child support orders. In FY2010, the CSE system handled 15.9 million cases, of which 86% (13.7 million) were non-TANF cases. In FY2010, the CSE program expenditures amounted to nearly $5.8 billion and the program collected $4.88 in child support payments (from noncustodial parents) for every dollar spent on the program.

---

* This is an edited, reformatted and augmented version of the Congressional Research Service Publication, CRS Report for Congress RL33422, dated July 19, 2012.

The federal government bears the majority of CSE program expenditures and provides incentive payments to the states for success in meeting CSE goals. Most child support collections for TANF families are kept by the federal government and states to reimburse themselves for the cost of providing TANF cash payments to those families. Collections for non-TANF families generally are paid to the families (via the state CSE disbursement unit).

Some policymakers are concerned that the federal government's role in financing CSE is too high, and contend that the states should pay a greater share of the program's costs. Comparing CSE expenditures with the income generated by retained collections for TANF families, the federal government has lost money each year since 1979 (the FY2009 "loss" to the federal government was $2.9 billion). Although in the past the income generated by the CSE program for states (in the aggregate) exceeded their expenses, this no longer holds true (the FY2009 "loss" to states was $718 million). The increasing federal "losses" on the CSE program and the switch from "gain" to "loss" for the state governments is in part attributable to the decline in the TANF caseload.

An alternative analysis views retained child support collections as reimbursement for a portion of cash welfare expenditures for families with children, rather than as "income" to the state. The share of AFDC/TANF cash expenditures reimbursed by child support collections grew consistently during the period from FY1994 through FY2002, when CSE collections for welfare families remained relatively stable, while cash welfare payments decreased dramatically, from $22.7 billion in FY1994 to $9.4 billion in FY2002. Between FY2002 and FY2010, AFDC/TANF cash expenditures fluctuated up and down. In FY1994, retained child support collections for welfare families as a percentage of total cash welfare expenditures was 11%; by FY2010, it was about 18% (after reaching a high point of nearly 31% in FY2002).

The change in the composition of the CSE caseload, together with changes made pursuant to P.L. 109-171, are expected to result in state CSE programs having to compete with all other state interests in obtaining funds from the general treasury or county treasuries. This is a dramatic departure from the past, when the CSE program was unique among social welfare programs in that it added money to state treasuries.

INTRODUCTION

This report describes the current system of child support financing, analyzes trends in child support collections and expenditures, and discusses the effect of declining Temporary Assistance for Needy Families (TANF)[1] rolls on Child Support Enforcement (CSE) program financing. It also explains how child support collections are distributed to families and to the state and federal governments. In addition, the report includes two appendices. **Appendix A** presents several state- by-state tables, which include an examination of state income and expenditures for every state for FY1999 and FY2009, collection and expenditure data by state for selected years from FY1999 to FY2010, average monthly child support payments in cases in which a collection was made for every state for selected years from FY1999 to FY2009, and child support collections made on behalf of TANF families as a percentage of total CSE collections for every state for selected years from FY1999 to FY2009. **Appendix B** describes the distribution of child support payments and the "family first" policy.

BACKGROUND

The CSE program was passed by Congress in 1975 (P.L. 93-647) with two primary goals. The first goal was to reduce public expenditures for actual and potential welfare recipients by obtaining ongoing support from noncustodial parents. The second goal was to establish paternity for children born outside marriage so that child support could be obtained. The December 1974 Finance Committee report on the CSE legislation stated, *"The problem of welfare in the United States is, to a considerable extent, a problem of the non-support of children by their absent parents."*[2] It also stated that the result of a new federal-state CSE program would be to lower welfare costs to the taxpayer and to deter fathers from abandoning their families.

Both welfare and nonwelfare families are eligible for CSE services. Although federal matching funds for CSE program expenditures on nonwelfare cases have been available to states since the program's enactment, they were authorized only on a temporary basis until 1980. P.L. 96-272 (enacted on June 17, 1980) made federal matching funds for CSE nonwelfare services available on a permanent basis.[3] Since 1989, nonwelfare families have exceeded welfare families in the CSE caseload.

States are responsible for administering the CSE program, but the federal government plays a major role in dictating the major design features of state programs, funding state and local programs, monitoring and evaluating state programs, providing technical assistance, and giving direct assistance to states in locating absent parents and obtaining child support payments.

All 50 states, the District of Columbia, Guam, Puerto Rico, and the Virgin Islands operate CSE programs and are entitled to federal matching funds.[4] To qualify for federal matching funds, each state's CSE plan must be approved by the Office of Child Support Enforcement (OCSE), Department of Health and Human Services (HHS).

The CSE program provides seven major services on behalf of children: parent location, paternity establishment, establishment of child support orders, review and modification of support orders, collection of support payments, distribution of support payments, and establishment and enforcement of medical child support orders.

Collection methods used by state CSE agencies include income withholding,[5] intercept of federal and state income tax refunds, intercept of unemployment compensation, liens against property, reporting child support obligations to credit bureaus, intercept of lottery winnings, sending insurance settlement information to CSE agencies, authority to withhold or suspend driver's licenses, professional licenses, and recreational and sporting licenses of persons who owe past- due support, and authority to seize assets of debtor parents held by public or private retirement funds and financial institutions. Moreover, federal law authorizes the Secretary of State to deny, revoke, or restrict passports of debtor parents. All jurisdictions also have civil or criminal contempt-of-court procedures and criminal nonsupport laws. In addition, federal criminal penalties may be imposed in certain cases. Federal law also requires states to enact and implement the Uniform Interstate Family Support Act (UIFSA), and expand full faith and credit procedures. Federal law also provides for international enforcement of child support.[6]

P.L. 104-193, the Personal Responsibility and Work Opportunity Reconciliation Act of 1996, replaced the Aid to Families with Dependent Children (AFDC) entitlement program with a TANF block grant and made major changes to the CSE program. P.L. 104-193 allowed all states to link up to an array of databases, and permitted the Federal Parent Locator Service (FPLS)[7] to be used for the purpose of establishing parentage; establishing, setting the amount of, modifying, or enforcing child support obligations; or enforcing child custody or visitation orders. It required that a designated state agency, directly or by contract, conduct automated comparisons of the Social

Security numbers reported by employers to the state directory of new hires[8] and the Social Security numbers of CSE cases that appear in the records of the state registry of child support orders. (The 1996 welfare reform law required the HHS Secretary to conduct similar comparisons of the federal directories.) When a match occurs, the state directory of new hires is required to report to the state CSE agency the name, date of birth, Social Security number of the employee, and employer's name, address, and identification number. The CSE agency then, within two business days, is required to instruct appropriate employers to withhold child support obligations from the employee's paycheck, unless the employee's income is not subject to withholding.[9] P.L. 104-193 required employers to remit to the state disbursement unit income withheld within seven business days after the employee's payday. P.L. 104-193 required states to operate a centralized collection and disbursement unit to send child support payments to custodial parents within two business days.

P.L. 104-193 also established what is often referred to as the "family first" policy, wherein a family that is no longer receiving TANF benefits has first claim on all child support paid by the noncustodial parent. This means that the states not only pay current child support that is collected to former TANF families, but also pay a higher proportion of arrearages (i.e., collections on past- due child support payments) to former TANF families.

Among other things, P.L. 109-171 (a budget reconciliation measure, referred to as the Deficit Reduction Act (DRA) of 2005) made a number of changes to the CSE program. P.L. 109-171 reduced the federal matching rate for laboratory costs associated with paternity establishment from 90% to 66%, ended the federal matching of state expenditures of federal CSE incentive payments reinvested back into the program,[10] and required states to assess a $25 annual user fee for child support services provided to families with no connection to the welfare system.[11] P.L. 109-171 also simplified CSE distribution rules and extends the "families first" policy by providing incentives to states to encourage them to allow more child support to go to both former welfare families and families still on welfare. In addition, P.L. 109-171 revised some child support enforcement collection mechanisms and added others.

Since the 1996 welfare reform changes, the TANF rolls have decreased significantly. As of December 2011, there were about 2 million TANF families on the rolls per month, and 40% of those families consisted of child-only families; in FY1994, there were about 5 million cash welfare families.[12] Moreover, annual federal and state TANF expenditures have decreased from almost $23 billion in FY1994 to $9.6 billion in FY2011. Reduced cash welfare rolls have resulted in a reduced share of welfare families in the CSE caseload, which means that the CSE program has a lesser amount of welfare costs to recover.

CSE Caseload

The CSE program serves both TANF recipients[13] and non-TANF recipients. In FY2010, the CSE system handled 15.9 million cases, of which 6.9 million (43%) were families who had never been on TANF, 6.8 million (43%) were former-TANF families, and 2.2 million (14%) were families who were receiving TANF assistance[14] (see **Figure 1**). Former-TANF cases are families that are no longer on TANF, therefore they are really non-TANF cases.

OCSE defines a CSE "case" as a noncustodial parent (mother, father, or putative/alleged father) who is now or eventually may be obligated under law for the support of a child or children receiving services under the CSE program. If the noncustodial parent owes support for two children by different women, that would be considered two cases; if both children have the same mother, that would be considered one case.

The CSE program defines a *current assistance case* as one in which the children are (1) recipients of cash aid under TANF (Title IV-A of the Social Security Act) or (2) entitled to Foster Care maintenance payments (Title IV-E of the Social Security Act). In addition, the children's support rights have been assigned by a caretaker to the state, and a referral to the state CSE agency has been made. A *former assistance case* is defined as a case in which the children were formerly receiving TANF or foster care services. A *never assistance case* is defined as a case in which the children are receiving services under the CSE program, but are not currently eligible for and have not previously received assistance under TANF or foster care.

In FY1978, AFDC/TANF cases[15] comprised 85% of the CSE caseload, but dropped to 14% of the caseload in FY2010. Available data show that non-TANF cases increasingly are families who formerly received TANF.

In FY1999, OCSE started reporting data for the following categories: current assistance, former assistance, and never received assistance rather than by TANF and non-TANF. The data indicate that the number and percentage of CSE families who currently receive TANF has decreased over time, while the number and percentage of CSE families who formerly received TANF has increased. The data also show that the proportion of the CSE caseload composed of families who had never received TANF has remained relatively stable for the period FY1999-FY2010. The decline in TANF families since 1994, and the relative stability of the segment of the caseload that had never been on the TANF rolls, resulted in a smaller CSE caseload. In FY1999, the CSE caseload was 17.3 million families; by FY2010, it had dropped to 15.9 million families.

In FY2010, the largest group of families who were participating in the CSE program were families who had left the TANF rolls (i.e., former TANF families—43%.[16] Families who had never been on TANF represented 43% of the CSE caseload, and families who were currently receiving TANF benefits comprised 14% of the CSE caseload (see **Figure 1**).[17] Thus, although the majority of the CSE caseload is composed of non-TANF families (86%), most of them at some point in their lives received TANF/AFDC (57%). This is consistent with the expanded mission of the CSE program. The expectation is that as child support becomes a more consistent and stable income source/support, these former TANF families will never have to return to the TANF rolls, and families who never resorted to the TANF program will never have to do so.

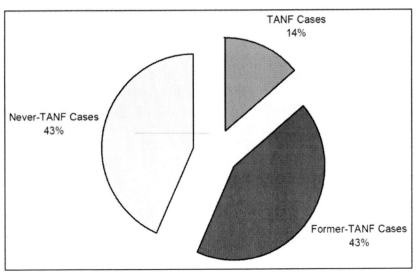

Source: Figure prepared by the Congressional Research Service (CRS) based on data from the Department of Health and Human Services (HHS).

Figure 1. Composition of Child Support Caseload, FY2010.

HOW THE CSE PROGRAM IS FINANCED

Context of the Current System

The CSE program is a federal-state matching grant program under which states must spend money in order to receive federal funding. For every dollar a state spends on CSE expenditures, it generally receives 66 cents from the federal government. States also receive CSE incentive payments from the federal government.[18] Although the actual dollars contributed by the federal government are greater than those from state treasuries, the level of funding allocated by the state or local government determines the total amount of resources available to the CSE agency.

One of the original goals of the CSE program was to reduce public expenditures on the AFDC program by obtaining child support from noncustodial parents on an ongoing basis. Thus, when the CSE program was enacted in 1975, a new requirement for AFDC eligibility was added, mandating custodial parents to assign to the state their rights to collect child support payments. This assignment covered current support and any arrearages (past-due support), and lasted as long as the family received AFDC benefits. When the family stopped receiving AFDC, the assignment ended. The custodial parent regained her or his right to collect current child support. However, if there were arrearages (and they were paid), the state could claim those arrearages up to the amount paid out in AFDC benefits.

Readers should note that the child support payments made on behalf of TANF children are paid to the state for distribution rather than directly to the family. If the child support collected is insufficient to lift the family's income above the state's TANF eligibility limit, the family receives its full TANF grant (i.e., not reduced by the child support payment), and the child support is collected by the state and distributed to the state treasury and the federal government in proportion to their assistance to the family. If the family's income, including the child support payments, exceeds the state's TANF eligibility limit, the family's TANF cash benefits are ended and all current child support payments are then sent directly to the family (via the state's child support disbursement unit).

As mentioned above, when the CSE program was first enacted in 1975, one of its primary goals was to recover the costs of providing cash welfare to families with children. To accomplish this cost-recovery goal, child support collected on behalf of families receiving AFDC directly offset AFDC benefit costs, and was shared between the federal and state governments in accordance with the matching formula used for the given state's AFDC program. Under old AFDC law, the rate at which states reimbursed the federal government for child support was the federal matching rate (i.e., the federal medical assistance percentage, or "Medicaid matching rate") for the AFDC program, which varied inversely with state per capita income (i.e., poor states have a high federal matching rate; wealthy states have a lower federal matching rate). In a state that had a 50% matching rate, the federal government was reimbursed $50 for each $100 collected in child support on behalf of an AFDC family, while in a state that had a 70% federal matching rate, the federal government was reimbursed $70 for each $100 collected. In the first example, the state kept $50, and in the second example, the state kept $30. Thus, states with a larger federal medical assistance matching rate kept a smaller portion of the child support collections. The match ranged from a minimum of 50% to a statutory maximum of 83%. Although AFDC was replaced by the TANF block grant under the welfare reform law of 1996, the same matching rate procedure is still used.

In terms of CSE collections, this cost-recovery procedure means that poorer states are rewarded less for their CSE efforts than wealthier states. In other words, states that are entitled to a relatively small proportion of child support collections because of paying a smaller share of AFDC benefit costs have to collect more child support payments per administrative dollar than other states to recover their costs (other things being equal).

There has been movement away from the cost-recovery goal, in part because of the changing nature of the CSE program. As discussed earlier (in the Caseload section), the component of the caseload that is composed of TANF families is shrinking. Even though overall child support collections increased by 67% over the 11-year period FY1999-FY2010 (see **Table A-3**), child support collections made on behalf of TANF families decreased by 21% (see **Table A-4**). In FY2010, only 14% of the CSE caseload was composed of TANF families. Thus, the policy shift—from using the CSE program to recover welfare costs to using it as a mechanism to consistently and reliably get child support income to families—is not surprising. In FY2009, only 7% of CSE collections ($1.9 billion) were made on behalf of TANF families (see **Table A-7**); about 12% of that amount went to the families (pursuant to state child support "pass through" provisions), and the rest was divided between the state and federal governments to reimburse them for TANF benefits paid to the families. This meant that in FY2009, 92% of CSE collections ($24.3 billion) went to the families on the CSE rolls.[19] The comparable figure in FY1999 was

85% ($13.5 billion); and the comparable figure in FY1996 was 80% ($9.6 billion).

Funding Elements

The CSE program is funded with both state and federal dollars. There are five funding streams for the CSE program. First, states spend their own money to operate a CSE program; the level of funding allocated by the state and/or localities determines the amount of resources available to CSE agencies.

CSE FUNDING ELEMENTS

- State dollars
- Federal matching funds (i.e., 66% of general state CSE expenditures)
- Retained child support collections from noncustodial parents on behalf of welfare families
- Incentive payments to states
- Fees

Second, the federal government reimburses each state 66% of all allowable expenditures on CSE activities.[20] The federal government's funding is "open-ended" in that it pays its percentage of expenditures by matching the amounts spent by state and local governments with no upper limit or ceiling.

Third, states collect child support on behalf of families receiving TANF to reimburse themselves (and the federal government) for the cost of TANF cash payments to the family. Federal law requires families who receive TANF cash assistance to assign their child support rights to the state in order to receive TANF. In addition, such families must cooperate with the state if necessary to establish paternity and secure child support. Collections on behalf of families receiving TANF cash benefits are used to reimburse state and federal governments for TANF payments made to the family (i.e., child support payments go to the state instead of the family, except for amounts that states choose to "pass through" to the family as additional income that does not affect TANF eligibility or benefit amounts).[21] The formula for distributing the child support payments collected by the states on behalf of TANF families between the state and the federal government is still based on the old AFDC federal-state reimbursement rates described earlier, even though the AFDC entitlement program was replaced by the TANF block grant program. Under existing law, states have the option of giving some, all, or none of their share of child support payments collected on behalf of TANF families to the family.[22] Pursuant to P.L. 109-171 (effective October 1, 2008), states that choose to pass through some of the collected child support to the TANF family *do not* have to pay the federal government its share of such collections if the amount passed through to the family and disregarded by the state does not exceed $100 per month ($200 per month to a family with two or more children) in child support collected on behalf of a TANF (or foster care) family.

Fourth, the federal government provides states with an incentive payment to encourage them to operate effective programs. Federal law requires states to reinvest CSE incentive payments back into the CSE program or related activities. (Through FY2007, if incentive payments were reinvested in the CSE program, they were reimbursed at the CSE federal matching rate of 66%.) In FY2004, the statutorily set maximum incentive payment for all states was $454 million. Effective October 1, 2007 (i.e., FY2008), P.L. 109-171 prohibited federal matching of state expenditure of federal CSE incentive payments. This meant that beginning on the effective date, CSE incentive payments that were received by states and reinvested in the CSE program were no longer eligible for federal reimbursement. However, P.L. 111-5 (the American Recovery and Reinvestment Act of 2009) temporarily reinstated federal matching of incentive payments for FY2009 and FY2010. There is currently no federal match on incentive payments.

Fifth, application fees and costs recovered from nonwelfare families may help finance the CSE program. In the case of a nonwelfare family, the custodial parent can hire a private attorney or apply for CSE services. As one might expect, hiring a private attorney is more expensive than applying for services under the federal/state CSE program. The CSE agency must charge an application fee, not to exceed $25, for families not on welfare. The CSE agency may charge this fee to the applicant or the noncustodial parent, or pay the fee out of state funds. In addition, a state may at its option recover costs in excess of the application fee. Such recovery may be either from the custodial parent or the noncustodial parent. Such fees and costs recovered from nonwelfare cases must be subtracted from the state's total administrative costs before calculating the federal reimbursement amount (i.e., the 66% matching rate).[23] Effective October 1, 2006, P.L. 109-171 requires families that have never been on TANF to pay a $25 annual user fee when child support enforcement efforts on their behalf are successful (i.e., at least $500 annually is collected on their behalf).[24] Thus, it is likely that the amount collected through fees from non-TANF families—especially persons who have never been in the cash welfare caseload—will increase significantly.

CSE Collections and the "Family First" Policy

When the CSE program was first enacted in 1975, welfare cost recovery was one of the primary goals of the program. There has been movement away from this goal, in part because of the changing nature of the CSE program. As discussed earlier, the size of the component of the caseload that is composed of TANF families is shrinking. Thus, the share of collections that are retained by the state or federal government as reimbursement for cash assistance payments is also shrinking.

Figure 2 shows the distribution of child support collections for FY2010. The bulk of distributed collections (9 out of 10 dollars) are for nonwelfare families and are paid to families. Child support collections made on behalf of welfare families (1 out of 10 dollars) are split among the federal government (federal share), state governments (state share), and families. As shown in **Figure 2**, medical child support represented 1% of total distributed CSE collections in FY2010.[25]

The 1996 welfare reform law established a "family first" policy that required states to give child support *arrearage* payments collected on behalf of former welfare families to the family first, prior to any state or federal reimbursement.[26] Before the enactment of P.L. 104-193, these collections could either be sent on to the families or retained by the state and federal government as reimbursement for past cash welfare assistance (i.e., AFDC/TANF). This "family first" policy was intended to help former welfare families stay self-sufficient and enhance cooperation with CSE efforts. The CSE strategic plan for the period FY2005-FY2009 states the following:

> Child support is no longer primarily a welfare reimbursement, revenue-producing device for the Federal and State governments; it is a family-first program, intended to ensure families' self-sufficiency by making child support a more reliable source of income.[27]

> ## CSE Changes Made by P.L. 109-171 (Deficit Reduction Act of 2005)
>
> Reduces the federal matching rate for laboratory costs associated with paternity establishment from 90% to 66%
>
> Ends the federal matching of state expenditures of federal CSE incentive payments reinvested back into the program
>
> Requires states to assess a $25 annual user fee for child support services provided to families with no connection to the welfare system
>
> Simplifies CSE distribution rules and extends the "family first" policy by providing incentives to states to encourage them to allow more child support to go to both former welfare families and families still on welfare
>
> Revises some child support enforcement collection mechanisms and adds others

One of the goals of the 1996 welfare reform law with regard to CSE distribution provisions was to create a distribution priority that favored families once they leave the TANF rolls. This "family first" policy was further advanced by P.L. 109-171. Generally speaking, pursuant to P.L. 109-171, child support that accrues before a family receives TANF and after the family stops receiving TANF will go to the family, whereas child support that accrues while the family is receiving TANF goes to the state and federal governments. This additional family income is expected to reduce dependence on public assistance by both promoting exit from TANF and preventing entry and re-entry to TANF. (For more detailed information on the "family first" policy, see **Appendix B.**)

Concurrently, the rules regarding the distribution of arrearage payments to former TANF families first, rather than to the states or federal government, may also result in reduced collections to be kept by the states and federal government.[28] Further, the proportion of nonwelfare families receiving CSE services continues to increase. As mentioned earlier, collections made on behalf of nonwelfare families go directly to the family (usually through the disbursement unit). Thus, while both the federal and state governments pay their share of the administrative costs for these families, neither gets a share of *current* collections made to these families.

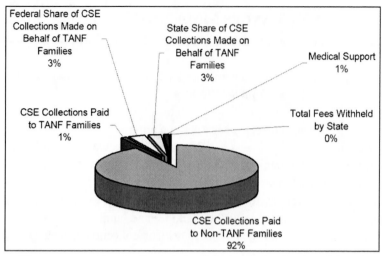

Source: Figure prepared by the Congressional Research Service (CRS) based on data
from the Department of Health and Human Services (HHS).

Figure 2. Percentages of Total Child Support Collections Distributed to Families, and
the Federal and State Governments, FY2010.

FINANCING ISSUES

Some policymakers view the federal reimbursement of state CSE
expenditures as too high. They contend that states should pay a higher
proportion of CSE costs. They assert that a less generous federal matching rate
would induce states to operate more efficiently. Others contend that states
faced with enforcing an array of federal laws and caseloads composed of a
larger share of nonwelfare families should not be confronted with higher CSE
costs. They also point out that the large interstate segment of the CSE program
demonstrates the need for relatively high federal funding. They support a
continuation of the federal financial commitment to the CSE program.

The National Governors' Association has argued that any reduction in the
federal government's financial commitment to the CSE system could
negatively affect states' ability to serve families. It contends that continued
implementation of CSE requirements without stable federal funding would
result in a significant cost shift to the states, which could jeopardize the
effectiveness of the CSE program and thereby could have a negative impact on
the children and families the CSE program is designed to serve.[29]

Expanded Mission

Many commentators agree that the mission of the CSE program has changed over the years. It began as a program to recover the costs of providing cash welfare to families with children, but the Child Support Enforcement Amendments of 1984 (P.L. 98-378) broadened the mission to reflect service delivery. In 1984, the criteria for making incentive payments to the states was broadened to include collections for nonwelfare families.

Some commentators assert that the service-delivery goal was reemphasized in the 1996 welfare reform legislation, which established the "family first" policy. To help assure that former welfare recipients stay off the TANF rolls, the family first policy requires that such families are to receive any child support arrearage payments collected by the state before the state and federal governments retain their share of collections. Additionally, the sharp decline in the TANF rolls and reduced expenditures on TANF have helped shift the program from recovering declining costs for a smaller population to collecting and paying child support to nonwelfare families.

Figure 3 and **Table 1** show the trend in child support collections for welfare and nonwelfare families from FY1979 through FY2010 in constant (inflation-adjusted) dollars. Collections for nonwelfare families increased in every year over this period, except for FY1982 and FY2010. Collections for welfare families increased in all but one year (FY1980) through FY1996, but have had several up and down fluctuations since FY1997. In real (inflation-adjusted) terms, nonwelfare collections increased almost elevenfold over the FY1979-FY2010 period, while collections for welfare families increased by 15%. It should be noted that the increase in nonwelfare collections is not merely the result of welfare families going off assistance and becoming nonwelfare families. In the early years of the program, many states failed to provide services to nonwelfare families. This changed over time, and for many years now, the nonwelfare portion of the CSE caseload has exceeded the welfare portion of the caseload.

Figure 3 and **Table 1** also show that from FY1980 through FY2008, total CSE collections, adjusted for inflation, had increased each year. In FY2009, total adjusted CSE collections decreased about 0.3% from their highest level in FY2008. In FY2010, total adjusted CSE collected decreased 1% from the FY2009 level and 1.3% from the FY2008 level.[30] The Office of Child Support Enforcement (OCSE) attributed the decrease in collections to the downturn in the U.S. economy during FY2009.[31]

Table 1.Welfare and Nonwelfare Collections, FY1979-2010
(in constant 2010 dollars)

	Welfare CSE Collections	Non-Welfare CSE Collections	Total CSE Collections
1979	$ 1,674,053,869	$ 2,066,328,335	$3,740,382,203
1980	1,519,309,951	2,203,084,329	3,722,394,280
1981	1,542,657,812	2,204,344,671	3,747,002,483
1982	1,705,299,293	2,136,701,542	3,842,000,835
1983	1,830,616,065	2,380,844,083	4,211,460,148
1984	1,999,045,377	2,753,562,099	4,752,607,476
1985	2,105,934,337	3,099,060,628	5,204,994,964
1986	2,326,024,286	3,840,131,838	6,166,156,123
1987	2,494,965,719	4,660,055,670	7,155,021,389
1988	2,631,018,581	5,524,551,573	8,155,570,154
1989	2,704,666,243	6,192,812,311	8,897,478,554
1990	2,830,252,652	6,889,151,515	9,719,404,167
1991	3,097,340,967	7,652,416,243	10,749,757,210
1992	3,439,286,014	8,687,389,898	12,126,675,913
1993	3,590,392,942	9,644,267,986	13,234,660,928
1994	3,709,319,876	10,620,625,203	14,329,945,079
1995	3,820,511,617	11,560,406,189	15,380,917,806
1996	3,950,700,662	12,681,695,353	16,632,396,015
1997	3,850,365,720	14,250,919,536	18,101,285,255
1998	3,539,872,613	15,626,317,121	19,166,189,734
1999	3,247,423,280	17,559,951,402	20,807,374,683
2000	3,283,141,877	19,322,384,977	22,605,526,854
2001	3,191,565,499	20,155,444,480	23,347,009,978
2002	3,506,330,584	20,898,759,636	24,405,090,220
2003	3,523,562,444	21,580,769,433	25,104,331,878
2004	2,612,859,237	22,621,369,646	25,234,228,883
2005	2,447,094,964	23,246,950,442	25,694,045,406
2006	2,283,623,752	23,597,732,678	25,881,356,431
2007	2,156,091,701	23,980,187,018	26,136,278,719
2008	2,282,740,671	24,613,963,998	26,896,704,669
2009	2,003,373,488	24,817,791,030	26,821,164,518
2010	1,925,379,969	24,630,361,054	26,555,741,023

Source: Table prepared by the Congressional Research Service (CRS) based on data from the Department of Health and Human Services (HHS), Office of Child Support Enforcement Annual Reports. Data were converted to constant dollars using CPI-U-RS (all items).

(in constant 2010 dollars)

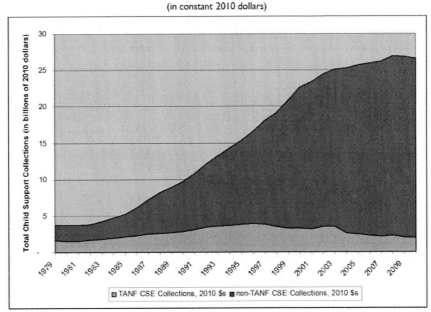

Source: Figure prepared by the Congressional Research Service (CRS) based on data from the Department of Health and Human Services (HHS).

Figure 3.Welfare and Nonwelfare Collections, FY1979-FY2010.

Revenue Gains and Losses

The child support program generates both income and expenditures for both the federal government and the states. States make expenditures to administer the program, but receive from the federal government both partial reimbursement for these costs and incentive payments. States also retain a share of collections made by noncustodial parents on behalf of welfare and foster care families. The federal government pays the above-mentioned share of state CSE expenditures and all incentive payments, but also retains a share of child support collections made on behalf of welfare families.

The income and outgo of the child support program can be examined from at least two different perspectives. The first shows how the CSE program by itself affects the cash flow of both federal and state budgets. However, collections retained to reimburse the federal government and the states for welfare and foster care costs represent *some* of the child support "income" for the states and *all* of the child support income for the federal government.

Another view of child support finances looks at collections as *reimbursement* for a state's welfare and foster care costs, rather than as child support income.

Cash Flow Generated by the Child Support Program

One perspective on the revenue gains and losses generated by the child support program compares expenditures with the income generated by retained child support collections and, for states, the federal reimbursement for certain expenditures and incentive payments. On this basis, the federal budget has been negatively affected by the CSE program for each year since 1979, as the federal share of state CSE expenditures and federal incentive payments to the states have exceeded the federal share of collections for TANF and foster care families. On the other hand, state budgets (in aggregate) were positively affected by the CSE program for the first 24 years of the program, in the sense that the income generated by the CSE program for the state (the federal share of state CSE expenditures—i.e., the amount of federal matching funds provided to the state—plus incentive payments to the states, plus the state share of child support collections made on behalf of TANF and foster care families) exceeded CSE program costs.

In FY1999, federal child support enforcement outgo exceeded income by $1.795 billion. In that year, state child support enforcement income exceeded outgo by $87 million (see **Table 2**). Since FY2000, both the federal government and the states have "lost" money on the CSE program. **Table 2** and **Figure 4** show the trends in the difference between income and outgo generated by the CSE program for both federal and state governments.[32] **Table 3** shows the long-term trend for the period FY1979-FY2009 in dollars adjusted for inflation (constant 2009 dollars).

The increasing federal "losses" on the CSE program and the switch from "gain" to "loss" for the state governments are in part attributable to the decline in the AFDC/TANF caseload. **Table 3** shows that when inflation is taken into account, the "gain" to the states dropped from $658 million in FY1997 to $379 million in FY1998 and to $112 million in FY1999; since FY2000, the states in aggregate have experienced a "loss" on the CSE program. In FY2000, state "losses" attributable to the CSE program amounted to $47 million, and have increased each year from FY2000 through FY2008; in FY2009, state "losses" amounted to $718 million. In other words, beginning in FY2000, almost all of the states have had to pay out more to operate their CSE programs than they received back in recovered welfare payments, incentive payments, and federal matching funds.[33]

Table 2. Federal, State, and Taxpayer "Savings" or "Costs" from Income and Expenditures Generated by the Child Support Enforcement (CSE) Program, FY1979-FY2009
(in current dollars)

	Federal CSE Costs	State CSE Savings or Costs	Taxpayer (Total Federal and State) CSE Savings/Costs
1979	-$42,601,000	$243,541,000	$200,940,000
1980	-102,698,000	230,152,000	127,454,000
1981	-128,376,000	260,968,000	132,592,000
1982	-147,869,000	307,378,000	159,509,000
1983	-138,078,000	312,296,000	174,218,000
1984	-105,049,000	365,523,000	260,474,000
1985	-230,888,000	317,335,000	86,447,000
1986	-264,338,000	273,782,000	9,444,000
1987	-337,278,000	351,345,850	14,067,850
1988	-355,424,000	381,000,764	25,576,764
1989	-480,056,000	372,529,985	-107,526,015
1990	-528,135,000	333,289,471	-194,845,529
1991	-602,591,000	401,249,537	-201,341,463
1992	-644,999,000	474,550,791	-170,448,209
1993	-764,544,000	486,539,478	-278,004,522
1994	-946,391,000	449,456,532	-496,934,468
1995	-1,273,306,000	408,421,381	-864,884,619
1996	-1,146,758,000	409,419,373	-737,338,627
1997	-1,281,773,000	493,678,078	-788,094,922
1998	-1,438,441,890	288,470,575	-1,149,971,315
1999	-1,795,452,888	87,339,827	-1,708,113,061
2000	-2,048,367,863	-37,759,819	-2,086,127,682
2001	-2,337,502,397	-185,991,554	-2,523,493,951
2002	-2,252,204,361	-351,107,650	-2,603,312,011
2003	-2,282,818,396	-357,033,610	-2,639,852,006
2004	-2,372,833,802	-422,292,852	-2,795,126,654
2005	-2,410,946,139	-455,471,924	-2,866,418,063
2006	-2,590,982,915	-550,989,358	-3,141,972,273
2007	-2,637,593,201	-578,905,889	-3,216,499,090
2008	-2,500,388,409	-788,664,948	-3,289,053,357
2009	-2,942,262,883	-718,262,504	-3,660,525,387

Source: Table prepared by the Congressional Research Service (CRS) based on data from the Department of Health and Human Services (HHS), Office of Child Support Enforcement Annual Reports.

Note: These numbers are in current dollars, and thereby do not take inflation into account.

(in millions of constant 2009 dollars)

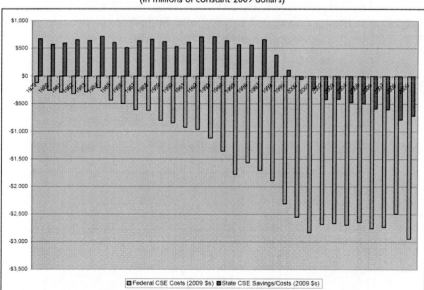

Source: Figure prepared by the Congressional Research Service (CRS) based on data
from the Department of Health and Human Services (HHS).

Figure 4. Federal and State "Savings" and/or "Costs" from Income and Expenditures
Generated by the Child Support Enforcement Program, FY1979-FY2009.

Table 3. Federal, State, and Taxpayer "Savings" or "Costs" from Income and Expenditures Generated by the Child Support Enforcement (CSE) Program, FY1979-FY2009 (in constant 2009 dollars)

	Federal CSE Costs	State CSE Savings/Costs	Taxpayer (Total Federal and State) CSE Savings/Costs
1979	-$117,610,123	$672,352,454	$554,742,331
1980	-254,522,974	570,400,315	315,877,341
1981	-290,506,034	590,552,586	300,046,552
1982	-315,574,085	655,989,634	340,415,549
1983	-282,615,789	639,202,339	356,586,550
1984	-206,557,022	718,725,000	512,167,978
1985	-438,924,080	603,262,070	164,337,990
1986	-493,577,178	511,211,203	17,634,025

	Federal CSE Costs	State CSE Savings/Costs	Taxpayer (Total Federal and State) CSE Savings/Costs
1987	-609,189,048	634,598,296	25,409,247
1988	-619,239,823	663,801,110	44,561,287
1989	-801,790,244	622,200,134	-179,590,110
1990	-840,214,773	530,233,249	-309,981,523
1991	-925,481,058	616,253,555	-309,227,503
1992	-966,118,331	710,810,743	-255,307,588
1993	-1,117,546,914	711,182,996	-406,363,918
1994	-1,354,444,184	643,247,649	-711,196,535
1995	-1,779,464,907	570,775,222	-1,208,689,685
1996	-1,561,057,779	557,334,064	-1,003,723,714
1997	-1,707,946,256	657,819,774	-1,050,126,482
1998	-1,890,317,878	379,091,494	-1,511,226,384
1999	-2,311,269,553	112,431,735	-2,198,837,819
2000	-2,551,347,872	-47,031,803	-2,598,379,675
2001	-2,831,974,058	-225,335,921	-3,057,309,979
2002	-2,685,255,010	-418,618,129	-3,103,873,140
2003	-2,662,302,091	-416,384,995	-3,078,687,086
2004	-2,694,457,994	-479,532,258	-3,173,990,252
2005	-2,648,929,312	-500,431,308	-3,149,360,620
2006	-2,756,364,803	-586,158,891	-3,342,523,695
2007	-2,728,544,691	-598,868,161	-3,327,412,852
2008	-2,490,899,269	-785,671,912	-3,276,571,181
2009	-2,942,262,883	-718,262,504	-3,660,525,387

Source: Table prepared by the Congressional Research Service (CRS) based on data from the Department of Health and Human Services (HHS), Office of Child Support Enforcement Annual Reports.

Note: Data were converted to constant dollars using CPI-U-RS (all items).

The cash flow for child support programs at the state level has implications for funding of the CSE program in some states. Some state administrators have "sold" their CSE program to their state legislatures on the basis that the child support program had added money to the state treasury, whereas most other social welfare programs reduced the state coffers. This meant that some state legislatures did not have to appropriate funds to pay for their CSE program. In FY2009, only five states (Alaska, Kentucky, Maine, Massachusetts, and Rhode Island) were able to make that argument.

Although in the aggregate, the income generated by the CSE program for states exceeded their outgo for the first 24 years of the program, this was not true for all states (and is no longer true in the aggregate). In FY1999, only 13 states experienced increased income from operating a CSE program (down from 41 states in FY1994); the other states and jurisdictions operated at a "loss." (See **Table A-1.**) In FY2009, the comparable number of states whose income exceeded outgo with respect to the CSE program fell to five. (See **Table A-2.**)

In the past, the states with income exceeding outgo tended to be high-income states with a relatively low federal medical assistance percentage (FMAP).[34] A poor state like Mississippi used to pay for about 20% of its AFDC benefit costs (the federal government paid for about 80% of the state's AFDC benefit costs). Therefore, the state got to "keep" only 20% of its child support collections made on behalf of welfare families. Mississippi has consistently "lost" money on the CSE program if its finances are viewed from the perspective of income and outgo generated by the program. On the other hand, New Hampshire used to pay about 47% of the AFDC benefit costs, and therefore got to keep 47% of its child support collections on behalf of welfare families. New Hampshire has consistently gained financially from operating a CSE program, when viewed from this perspective. Of course, New Hampshire bore a greater share of welfare expenditures than did Mississippi. When viewed from the perspective of child support collections as reimbursement for welfare costs, high-income states retain more of their collections because they paid for more of their welfare costs.[35]

An examination of FY2009 data indicates that the pattern of state income exceeding outgo primarily in states with a relatively low federal medical assistance percentage (FMAP) is not as clear as it was in the past. For example, although Massachusetts, with its relatively low FMAP of 50% in FY2009, gained financially from operating a CSE program, so too did the state of Kentucky, which had a relatively high FMAP of 70% in FY2009.

The last column of **Table A-2** shows a measure of CSE program effectiveness, obtained by dividing total state collections by total state administrative expenditures (costs). This measure is generally referred to as the collections-to-costs ratio. The table shows that in FY2009, $4.78 in child support was collected for every dollar spent on CSE activities (i.e., national average). In other words, for every dollar that was spent by federal, state, and local governments, $4.78 was collected by the states from noncustodial parents for the financial support of their children (i.e., private funds). The table shows that there were wide differences among states in how much child support was collected for each dollar spent on the CSE program, ranging from $2.03 in New Mexico to $9.80 in Texas. It is interesting to note that the collections-to-costs ratio did not seem to affect whether a state financially gained from operating a CSE program, given that both Maine (a state with a ratio that was below the national average) and Kentucky (a state with a ratio that was almost 57% higher than the national average) financially gained from operating a CSE program in FY2009.

Some analysts claim that the collections-to-costs or cost-effectiveness ratio indicate that states do not have an incentive to control their expenditures on the CSE program; these analysts further contend that the 66% reimbursement rate may provide states with an incentive to spend money inefficiently. Others maintain that although state finances are generally on more stable footing than they were during the past couple of years, state resources are still limited with respect to the many state programs and activities that need to be funded every year, and thus the nature of state budgets in and of themselves provides the incentive for states to keep CSE expenditures reasonable.

One explanation of why states have been consistently "losing" money on the CSE program in recent years is that nonwelfare collections are growing at a faster rate than welfare collections; child support collections on behalf of nonwelfare families increased by 82% over the period FY1999-FY2009 (see **Table A-5**), while child support collections on behalf of welfare families decreased by 21% over that period (see **Table A-4**). While the state and federal governments share in a portion of welfare collections, nonwelfare collections go exclusively to the custodial parent via the state disbursement unit.

Child Support Financing and Welfare Costs

An alternative analysis of the revenue gains and losses of the CSE program takes into account the consideration that child support collections retained by the federal government and states are offsets to expenditures on TANF cash benefits, rather than offsets to CSE programs. That is, it is possible to view retained child support collections as a method of financing a portion of a state's cash welfare expenditures rather than its child support expenditures. In a study for HHS, researchers surveyed states in 1998 and found that 25% of the states used their share of CSE collections to finance their TANF programs, rather than their CSE programs.[36] The states that used their collections to finance TANF expenditures included California and New York, the two largest states in terms of the TANF caseload and TANF expenditures.

Even though TANF is a block grant program with fixed grant amounts (i.e., no federal matching rate), federal law requires (1) families receiving "assistance" under state TANF programs to assign their child support to the state;[37] and (2) states to pay the federal government the federal share of child support collections made on behalf of TANF and former TANF families. As described earlier, the federal share is the formula used to determine the federal medical assistance percentage, the same formula that was used under prior law as the matching rate for AFDC and to divide child support enforcement collections.

Figure 5 compares total federal and state cash assistance (AFDC/TANF) payments with child support collections made on behalf of AFDC/TANF families for FY1994-FY2010. The share of AFDC/TANF cash expenditures reimbursed by child support collections grew consistently during the period from FY1994 through FY2002, when CSE collections for welfare families remained relatively stable, while cash welfare payments decreased dramatically, from $22.7 billion in FY1994 to $9.4 billion in FY2002. Between FY2002 and FY2010, AFDC/TANF cash expenditures fluctuated up and down. In FY1994, retained child support collections for welfare families as a percentage of total cash welfare expenditures was 11%; by FY2010, it was about 18%, after reaching a high point of nearly 31% in FY2002 (see **Figure 5**).

CSE Incentive System

P.L. 105-200, the Child Support Performance and Incentive Act of 1998 (enacted July 16, 1998), replaced the old incentive payment system[38] with a revised incentive payment system that provides (1) incentive payments based on a percentage of the state's collections (with no cap on non-TANF collections), (2) incorporation of five performance measures related to establishment of paternity and child support orders, collections of current and past-due support payments, and cost-effectiveness; (3) phase-in of the incentive system, with it being fully effective beginning in FY2002; (4) mandatory reinvestment of incentive payments into the CSE program; and (5) an incentive payment formula weighted in favor of TANF and former TANF families.

(in billions of dollars)

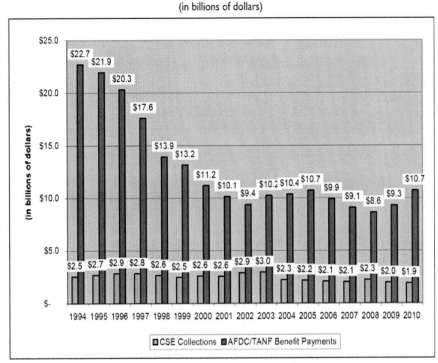

Source: Figure prepared by the Congressional Research Service (CRS) based on data from the Department of Health and Human Services (HHS).

Figure 5. Cash Welfare (AFDC/TANF) Payments and Child Support Collections Made on Behalf of AFDC/TANF Families, FY1994-FY2010.

The aggregrate incentive payment to states was $504 million in FY2009 and FY2010.[39] The CSE incentive payment system adds uncertainty to states' reliance on what used to be a somewhat predictable source of income. Although in the aggregate, states receive higher incentive payments than under the earlier incentive payment system, these totals are a fixed amount,[40] and individual states have to compete with each other for their share of the capped funds.

The CSE incentive payment system was fully implemented in FY2002. Pursuant to P.L. 105-200, the federal incentive pool was capped, thereby forcing states for the first time to compete against each other for incentive payment dollars. Under the revised incentive system, a state may be eligible to receive an incentive payment for good performance. The total amount of the incentive payment depends on four factors: the total amount of money available in a given fiscal year from which to make incentive payments, the state's success in making collections on behalf of its caseload, the state's performance in five areas (mentioned earlier), and the relative success or failure of other states in making collections and meeting these performance criteria.[41]

Moreover, unlike the old incentive system, which allowed states and counties to spend incentive payments on whatever they chose, the revised incentive system requires that the incentive payment be reinvested into either the CSE program or some other activity that might lead to improving the efficiency or effectiveness of the CSE program (e.g., mediation, parenting classes, efforts to improve the earning capacity of noncustodial parents, etc.).[42]

Welfare Cost Avoidance

Usual cost accounting overlooks savings from the avoidance of welfare payments. Many program analysts argue that indirect savings occur when child support collections keep a family off welfare, and that these savings make the CSE program worthwhile, despite the apparent loss under the current accounting system. Some analysts assert that although it is difficult to determine *how much* money might have been spent on various public assistance programs had it not been for the collection of child support payments, these indirect benefits of the CSE program should not be dismissed or ignored.[43]

Some observers argue that a strong CSE program encourages noncustodial parents to fulfill their child support obligation because they fear the consequences of not doing so. They contend that these child support payments reduce government spending by providing families with incomes sufficient enough to make them ineligible for programs such as TANF, food stamps, and Medicaid.

The indirect effects of changes in the CSE program on other programs are "scored" in cost estimates of legislation. That is, CBO estimates the impact of changes in the CSE program on outlays for programs such as Food Stamps and Medicaid. Some have argued that the budget itself ought to reflect welfare cost avoidance, by crediting the CSE budget account with these indirect savings from other programs. The budget would then reflect the *net* cost of the program to the federal government, after taking into account savings achieved in other programs. This can be viewed as preferable to showing the gross cost of the program for purposes of helping Congress and the President make decisions about the allocation of resources within the federal budget.

However, there are both practical and conceptual issues about explicitly including welfare cost avoidance in federal budgeting:

- On a practical level, it is difficult to reliably measure those who would be eligible for and are receiving TANF and other assistance programs in the absence of the CSE program. Doing so requires estimating what the world would look like under a counterfactual (i.e., what if the child support program did not exist), which requires making numerous assumptions. TANF "welfare" savings are generally redirected by states to other activities allowable under the block grant, as opposed to reduced state spending.
- Conceptually, the budget is meant to be a document that helps make decisions about both resource allocation *and* the federal government's fiscal policy. In terms of fiscal policy, attributing welfare cost avoidance "savings" to the child support enforcement program is simply a book-keeping transaction: it does nothing in and of itself to change the revenues to or the outlays from the federal government. It could be argued that complicating the accounting of child support obfuscates its fiscal impact, which is how much the program spends and how much it generates in collections (its transactions with the public). It could also be argued that policy makers routinely ignore such book-keeping rules, particularly when overall spending or deficit/surplus goals drive policy.

A report contracted by the federal Office of Child Support Enforcement (OCSE) entitled "Child Support Cost Avoidance in 1999, Final Report" concludes by stating the following:

> Unlike cost recovery, cost avoidance can only be estimated. It cannot be directly measured. But when even a lower-bound estimate of cost avoidance exceeds the total amount of cost recovery, it is clear that cost avoidance is an important part of the picture. As the child support enforcement community calls attention to child support's ability to improve families' financial stability and independence, it is worth recognizing that this increased independence also implies financial benefits to government through cost avoidance.[44]

Readers should note that the CSE program, unlike other social services programs, ensures the transfer of private—not public—funds to nonwelfare families enrolled in the program. Thus, as implied earlier, the CSE program imposes personal responsibility on noncustodial parents by requiring them to meet their financial obligations to their children, thereby alleviating taxpayers of this responsibility.

Maintaining the Cost-Effectiveness of the CSE Program

During the 32-year period between FY1978 and FY2010, child support payments collected by CSE agencies increased from $1 billion in FY1978 to $26.6 billion in FY2010, and the number of children whose paternity was established or acknowledged increased from 111,000 to 1.734 million. However, the program still collects only 19% of child support obligations for which it has responsibility if arrearage payments are taken into account (otherwise, 62%) and collects payments for only 56% of its caseload. In FY2010, $142.9 billion in child support obligations ($32.6 billion in current support and $110.3 billion in past-due support) was owed to families receiving CSE services, but only $27.6 billion was paid ($20.2 billion current, $7.4 billion past- due).

During the period between FY1978 and FY2010, total expenditures on CSE activities increased from $312 million in FY1978 to $5.776 billion in FY2010. (See **Appendix A** for state information on CSE collections and expenditures for selected years during the period FY1999- FY2010.) OCSE data indicate that in FY2010, paternity had been established or acknowledged for 92% of the 11.2 million children on the CSE caseload without legally identified fathers. In FY2010, the CSE program collected $4.88 in child support payments (from noncustodial parents) for every dollar spent on the program.[45]

Many child support advocates are concerned that reductions in federal financing of the CSE program will result in a less cost-effective program. They argue that it does not make sense to hamper a successful program.

Some advocates of children maintain that CSE funding cuts will erode the tremendous progress made by the states in making their CSE programs more efficient and effective, and that this could result in fewer noncustodial parents supporting their children and more families enrolling in welfare programs.[46] Many advocates of children agree that as CSE federal funding is reduced, states will be forced to cut back on their CSE funding as well because of reduced resources. They argue that the likely result will be fewer enforcement actions directed toward the more difficult and costly cases, and thus they contend that low-income children could bear the brunt of the CSE funding reductions and could receive much less of the child support they are owed.[47]

As mentioned earlier in the report, P.L. 109-171 eliminated the federal match on CSE incentive payments beginning with FY2008, but P.L. 111-5 reinstated the federal match on CSE incentive payment for FY2009 and FY2010. According to a 2011 Government Accountability Office (GAO) report:

> Several state officials we interviewed confirmed that they were using the reinstated incentive match funds to sustain program operations and avoid layoffs during tight state budget climates. This is unlike prior years, when incentive match funds might have been used for long-term projects because funding was more predictable. Looking to the future, several of the state officials we interviewed described funding uncertainty surrounding the expiration of the incentive match in fiscal year 2011, as well as state budget situations. Not knowing whether the incentive match will be extended again or how much their future state CSE appropriations will be has made planning more difficult.
>
> Several officials emphasized that even states that maintained overall expenditure levels when the incentive match was eliminated in fiscal year 2008 may not be able to do so again in fiscal year 2011, as many state budget situations have worsened since the economic recession. Some officials also noted that the delivery of services beyond the core mission of the CSE program—such as job skills training and fatherhood initiatives—is particularly uncertain.
>
> These officials also told us that, although they believe that these services and partnerships are necessary to continue increasing their collections, particularly from noncustodial parents who are underemployed or have barriers to maintaining employment, these services would be reduced to preserve core services in the event of dramatic budget shortfalls.[48]

Financing the State and Local Share of Child Support Expenditures

As noted earlier, enactment of P.L. 109-171 (February 8, 2006) gave states the option of implementing a "family-first" policy. Acceptance of a family-first policy raises some concerns regarding the funding of the CSE program.

Under a family-first policy, more child support dollars would go to families (both TANF families and non-TANF families), and thereby less money would go to the states and the federal government for reimbursement of cash welfare assistance to the family.

Also, pursuant to P.L. 109-171, states are no longer entitled to receive federal matching funds for CSE incentive payments that the state reinvests in the CSE program (effective October 1, 2007, i.e. FY2008). Thus, one source of funding, federal matching of incentive payments, was totally eliminated,[49] and another source of funding (the state share of retained child support payments collected on behalf of TANF families) probably will continue to decline.

The elimination of federal reimbursement of CSE incentive payments may result in a significant reduction in CSE financing in the future. Before FY2008 and in FY2009 and FY2010, the federal match resulted in a near tripling of state CSE funding/expenditures. For example, in FY2009, actual incentive payments to states amounted to $504 million; the federal match (at the 66% rate) on the incentive payments amounted to almost twice that figure, $978 million, which translates into the state spending $1.482 billion on CSE activities.[50]

The CSE program used to be unique in that it was a social welfare program that added money to state treasuries, this is no longer the case, with the exception of a handful of states. State CSE programs are now in the position of having to compete with all other state interests in obtaining funds from the general treasury or county treasuries.

The Deficit Reduction Act of 2005 (P.L. 109-171) made changes to the CSE program that have resulted in less federal financial support to state CSE programs.

The Deficit Reduction Act provisions together with a congruence of several program factors and policies (i.e., reduced percentage of cash welfare families on the CSE rolls and commitment to allow former welfare families to keep a greater portion of child support collected from noncustodial parents) may mean that states will have to increase state funding in order for CSE programs to continue to run effectively.

APPENDIX A. STATE-BY-STATE FINANCING INFORMATION

Table A-1. Financing of the Federal-State Child Support Enforcement Program, FY1999

State	Federal Share of CSE Expenditures	State Share of Collections	Federal Incentive Payments	State CSE Expenditures	State Net (Savings or Costs)	Collections to Costs Ratio
Alabama	$35,611,163	$5,241,898	$2,925,629	$53,533,869	-$9,755,179	$3.78
Alaska	11,892,504	8,124,670	2,683,407	17,964,120	$4,736,461	4.41
Arizona	38,907,328	7,908,214	3,978,350	58,657,247	-$7,863,355	3.29
Arkansas	24,408,488	2,678,949	2,072,889	36,804,856	-$7,644,530	3.28
California	405,195,689	298,330,943	82,935,948	612,709,196	$173,753,384	2.78
Colorado	34,459,151	14,837,153	5,377,881	51,970,056	$2,704,129	3.65
Connecticut	25,500,777	23,648,357	7,570,416	38,575,967	$18,143,583	4.96
Delaware	12,097,749	3,071,513	981,294	18,204,947	-$2,054,391	2.97
District of Columbia	8,761,188	2,507,042	829,254	13,240,866	-$1,143,382	3.27
Florida	126,081,489	32,227,673	13,486,222	190,501,671	-$18,706,287	3.53
Georgia	59,553,919	13,972,035	7,399,714	89,929,572	-$9,003,904	4.16
Guam	2,518,316	579,865	212,137	3,803,786	-$493,468	2.25
Hawaii	13,853,295	4,259,798	1,524,364	20,129,474	-$492,017	3.25
Idaho	6,933,950	1,220,776	926,483	10,486,201	-$1,404,992	7.09
Illinois	91,778,835	35,626,059	10,783,073	138,846,999	-$659,032	2.52
Indiana	25,536,707	7,366,308	3,948,769	38,548,504	-$1,696,720	7.45
Iowa	28,716,250	15,577,006	6,357,855	42,592,938	$8,058,173	5.01
Kansas	32,764,235	11,286,869	4,301,156	49,627,981	-$1,275,721	2.98

Table A-1. (Continued)

State	Federal Share of CSE Expenditures	State Share of Collections	Federal Incentive Payments	State CSE Expenditures	State Net (Savings or Costs)	Collections to Costs Ratio
Kentucky	37,249,397	10,425,186	5,070,254	56,187,842	-$3,443,005	3.9
Louisiana	31,631,370	5,188,683	2,573,418	47,330,767	-$7,937,296	4.41
Maine	12,331,480	8,957,322	4,352,601	18,622,365	$7,019,038	4.87
Maryland	54,963,710	12,142,185	3,487,062	82,662,138	-$12,069,181	4.42
Massachusetts	50,191,367	26,955,285	7,003,813	75,075,897	$9,074,568	4.07
Michigan	108,662,792	56,952,941	16,937,698	164,473,879	$18,079,552	7.81
Minnesota	74,863,180	27,771,128	8,416,633	113,148,820	-$2,097,879	4.06
Mississippi	20,364,999	2,399,038	1,937,334	30,617,658	-$5,916,287	4.53
Missouri	62,432,181	13,358,740	5,601,102	94,391,679	-$12,999,656	3.26
Montana	7,776,191	1,573,860	968,243	11,640,510	-$1,322,216	3.87
Nebraska	21,194,022	4,668,984	2,800,715	31,973,151	-$3,309,430	3.61
Nevada	25,118,585	3,552,729	2,049,489	38,022,688	-$7,301,885	3.08
New Hampshire	11,465,868	4,035,135	1,343,250	16,919,544	-$75,291	4.24
New Jersey	91,926,796	35,984,052	10,384,931	139,127,636	-$831,857	4.86
New Mexico	21,372,665	2,738,442	1,524,652	32,341,992	-$6,706,233	1.18
New York	140,805,327	88,099,847	26,353,184	212,809,547	$42,448,811	4.58
North Carolina	86,026,282	15,263,427	6,565,419	130,060,394	-$22,205,266	2.93
North Dakota	6,840,076	1,433,106	832,665	9,957,810	-$851,963	4.42
Ohio	181,533,385	35,691,105	13,003,442	274,378,160	-$44,150,228	4.91
Oklahoma	21,367,112	5,982,850	3,243,588	32,252,862	-$1,659,312	3.37
Oregon	27,941,846	9,165,538	4,673,083	42,336,273	-$555,806	6.08

State	Federal Share of CSE Expenditures	State Share of Collections	Federal Incentive Payments	State CSE Expenditures	State Net (Savings or Costs)	Collections to Costs Ratio
Pennsylvania	122,633,135	40,339,166	12,683,050	183,526,973	-$7,871,622	6.21
Puerto Rico	19,678,756	519,976	384,110	29,797,384	-$9,214,542	5.77
Rhode Island	7,458,854	8,153,600	2,888,831	10,920,203	$7,581,082	4.36
South Carolina	24,393,946	3,244,212	2,331,956	36,672,072	-$6,701,958	5.06
South Dakota	4,422,754	1,499,266	2,290,352	6,554,522	$1,657,850	6.75
Tennessee	34,897,180	5,971,748	3,886,480	52,191,331	-$7,435,923	4.69
Texas	135,875,645	40,379,443	13,965,567	202,946,289	-$12,725,634	4.23
Utah	24,222,336	5,455,212	3,132,907	36,312,567	-$3,502,112	3.24
Vermont	6,065,541	2,670,478	1,176,980	9,047,583	$865,416	4.15
Virgin Islands	1,693,368	105,345	57,285	2,559,423	-$703,425	2.86
Virginia	50,303,090	17,724,145	6,332,102	75,708,963	-$1,349,626	4.74
Washington	78,023,327	45,326,692	13,956,503	118,133,123	$19,173,399	4.68
West Virginia	18,986,263	1,338,056	4,223,837	28,668,536	-$4,120,380	4.09
Wisconsin	64,579,502	13,523,868	5,162,502	96,688,882	-$13,423,010	5.64
Wyoming	5,900,784	1,330,007	633,827	8,764,286	-$899,668	4.84
Total	$2,679,764,145	$1,048,385,925	$360,523,706	$4,038,951,999	$49,721,777	$4.21

Source: Table prepared by the Congressional Research Service based on data from the Department of Health and Human Services, Office of Child Support Enforcement.

Note: The "State Net" total of $49.7 million in this table differs from the state total for FY1999 in **Table 3** ($87.3 million) because a hold harmless payment (from the federal government) in the amount of $37.6 million was paid to the states in FY1999—$49.7 million + $37.6 million = $87.3 million.

Table A-2. Financing of the Federal-State Child Support Enforcement Program, FY2009

State	Federal Share of CSE Expenditures	State Share of Collections	Federal Incentive Payments (Actual)	State Expenditures	State Net (Savings or Costs)	Collections-to-Costs Ratio
Alabama	$45,119,205	$3,761,226	$4,563,098	$68,362,430	-$14,918,901	$4.27
Alaska	16,086,290	6,669,013	1,954,695	24,373,167	$336,831	4.5
Arizona	47,592,246	8,502,784	6,488,968	72,109,458	-$9,525,460	4.97
Arkansas	32,043,040	2,019,536	4,722,610	48,550,063	-$9,764,877	4.6
California	704,967,633	205,176,174	37,681,286	1,067,826,279	-$120,001,186	2.1
Colorado	45,448,874	8,596,399	5,513,994	68,861,928	-$9,302,661	4.56
Connecticut	49,510,406	17,557,625	5,309,139	75,015,770	-$2,638,600	3.62
Delaware	19,498,553	2,536,447	1,276,175	29,543,265	-$6,232,090	2.78
District of Columbia	19,467,809	2,944,213	938,962	29,496,682	-$6,145,698	2.02
Florida	202,417,603	26,751,866	28,316,508	293,701,984	-$36,216,007	4.85
Georgia	59,773,108	9,346,065	9,742,854	90,565,314	-$11,703,287	7.22
Guam	3,067,598	361,048	198,122	4,647,876	-$1,021,108	2.87
Hawaii	14,667,411	4,501,028	1,746,576	22,223,352	-$1,308,337	4.72
Idaho	20,674,142	1,055,693	2,726,398	31,324,457	-$6,868,224	4.85
Illinois	127,229,889	16,079,734	13,773,404	188,957,015	-$31,873,988	4.65
Indiana	52,712,740	9,690,912	12,565,043	78,903,001	-$3,934,306	7.73
Iowa	40,496,026	12,626,397	7,785,162	61,357,617	-$450,032	5.61
Kansas	39,097,594	9,077,922	4,102,207	59,238,779	-$6,961,056	3.44
Kentucky	38,487,015	11,245,672	8,077,059	54,834,442	$2,975,304	7.51

State	Federal Share of CSE Expenditures	State Share of Collections	Federal Incentive Payments (Actual)	State Expenditures	State Net (Savings or Costs)	Collections-to-Costs Ratio
Louisiana	51,533,965	3,933,172	7,459,128	78,081,763	-$15,155,498	4.66
Maine	18,652,065	7,869,479	2,150,433	28,260,704	$411,273	3.85
Maryland	72,193,708	10,706,100	7,700,541	109,384,405	-$18,784,056	4.8
Massachusetts	53,662,329	20,218,788	10,407,451	81,306,559	$2,982,009	7.04
Michigan	159,793,467	35,431,120	27,212,268	242,111,314	-$19,674,459	5.89
Minnesota	109,758,302	18,501,292	12,490,616	166,300,457	-$25,550,247	3.72
Mississippi	20,117,291	1,684,267	3,909,441	30,480,739	-$4,769,740	8.74
Missouri	61,290,688	15,818,582	12,217,568	92,864,679	-$3,537,841	6.28
Montana	9,466,136	1,415,447	1,133,891	14,342,628	-$2,327,154	4.36
Nebraska	27,422,135	3,057,004	3,323,105	41,548,687	-$7,746,443	4.83
Nevada	31,084,731	4,242,063	2,706,815	47,098,081	-$9,064,472	3.88
New Hampshire	12,875,271	3,534,917	1,796,373	19,507,988	-$1,301,427	4.53
New Jersey	193,697,172	25,902,965	17,044,615	293,480,561	-$56,835,809	3.85
New Mexico	32,605,349	2,470,667	1,599,902	50,605,839	-$13,929,921	2.03
New York	245,851,771	45,404,377	28,206,904	372,652,679	-$53,189,627	4.67
North Carolina	89,085,124	9,144,760	15,207,862	134,977,461	-$21,539,715	5.21
North Dakota	9,845,284	1,945,119	1,975,627	14,912,385	-$1,146,355	5.86
Ohio	234,859,908	28,343,524	29,511,680	355,913,044	-$63,197,932	4.95
Oklahoma	46,893,937	5,993,648	5,778,194	71,051,422	-$12,385,643	4.13
Oregon	43,925,887	8,466,398	6,264,490	66,554,377	-$7,897,602	5.46
Pennsylvania	161,731,302	23,042,904	26,009,432	246,948,495	-$36,164,857	5.98

Table A-2. (Continued)

State	Federal Share of CSE Expenditures	State Share of Collections	Federal Incentive Payments (Actual)	State Expenditures	State Net (Savings or Costs)	Collections-to-Costs Ratio
Puerto Rico	28,214,723	420,271	4,200,924	42,749,576	-$9,913,658	8.02
Rhode Island	5,465,327	2,777,997	1,313,096	8,280,798	$1,275,622	7.87
South Carolina	34,981,145	2,727,222	4,505,379	53,001,735	-$10,787,989	4.83
South Dakota	6,177,028	1,140,237	1,810,652	9,359,132	-$231,215	9.15
Tennessee	49,745,386	9,435,198	10,180,983	75,371,798	-$6,010,231	7.51
Texas	202,012,482	24,448,538	53,403,514	286,966,470	-$7,101,936	9.8
Utah	30,022,172	3,391,291	3,546,019	45,488,139	-$8,528,657	3.96
Vermont	9,361,280	1,702,442	982,039	14,183,760	-$2,137,999	3.51
Virgin Islands	3,854,820	63,672	112,137	5,840,632	-$1,810,003	1.9
Virginia	59,221,347	17,516,229	11,570,363	89,729,317	-$1,421,378	7.16
Washington	99,518,269	26,146,833	11,306,412	148,460,009	-$11,488,495	4.61
West Virginia	26,679,037	2,170,229	4,200,568	40,422,780	-$7,372,946	4.93
Wisconsin	60,930,949	11,854,244	13,956,243	92,319,622	-$5,578,186	6.82
Wyoming	6,504,595	1,231,544	1,323,075	9,855,448	-$796,234	6.81
Total	$3,887,391,564	$740,652,294	$504,000,000	$5,850,306,362	-$718,262,504	$4.78

Source: Table prepared by the Congressional Research Service based on data from the Department of Health and Human Services, Office of Child Support Enforcement.

Table A-3.Trend in Total CSE Collections, by State, FY1999-FY2010 (in millions of dollars)

State	1999	2000	2005	2009	2010	Percent Change 1999-2010
Alabama	$185.9	$192.1	$237.3	$266.0	$268.4	44%
Alaska	67.1	71.1	85.1	96.5	93.4	39%
Arizona	169.2	196.8	266.6	314.8	326.9	93%
Arkansas	108.5	120.5	155.1	202.0	206.6	90%
California	1,604.2	2,059.5	2,222.0	2,145.4	2,151.5	34%
Colorado	163.5	176.1	236.3	281.3	282.6	73%
Connecticut	175.5	190.8	235.4	253.3	250.4	43%
Delaware	45.0	49.0	66.5	73.6	72.8	62%
District of Columbia	35.1	35.0	48.0	52.7	50.7	45%
Florida	579.8	648.0	1,076.7	1,289.3	1,358.1	134%
Georgia	330.6	361.9	498.9	589.0	603.4	83%
Guam	7.7	7.7	8.9	12.4	12.0	56%
Hawaii	60.5	66.5	83.6	98.6	94.9	57%
Idaho	64.3	75.1	115.5	141.0	145.2	126%
Illinois	325.6	361.3	561.8	796.9	798.9	145%
Indiana	271.1	366.2	481.2	604.3	596.0	120%
Iowa	201.2	218.7	289.9	328.5	320.8	59%
Kansas	138.0	139.2	152.6	181.2	177.9	29%
Kentucky	206.2	226.4	336.6	393.6	393.5	91%
Louisiana	188.1	213.9	289.3	339.5	349.2	86%

Table A-3. (Continued)

State	1999	2000	2005	2009	2010	Percent Change 1999-2010
Maine	80.7	89.4	100.8	103.7	101.7	26%
Maryland	350.2	367.9	453.4	489.6	484.9	38%
Massachusetts	291.5	318.6	466.0	547.0	563.6	93%
Michigan	1,274.6	1,347.4	1,381.5	1,391.9	1,310.6	3%
Minnesota	442.7	477.4	569.0	598.1	584.3	32%
Mississippi	128.9	144.4	195.3	253.8	265.2	106%
Missouri	285.8	339.0	467.5	554.4	560.2	96%
Montana	38.2	40.8	46.8	54.4	56.2	47%
Nebraska	110.6	142.5	159.2	188.8	190.5	72%
Nevada	92.1	79.3	115.5	153.9	159.2	73%
New Hampshire	66.2	71.4	80.8	82.4	82.2	24%
New Jersey	635.1	679.2	915.5	1,075.2	1,091.6	72%
New Mexico	34.9	39.5	68.4	92.2	8.6	183%
New York	909.8	1,102.0	1,400.1	1,622.6	1,626.9	79%
North Carolina	348.0	395.6	565.1	655.2	654.7	88%
North Dakota	40.9	41.8	63.0	79.1	82.3	101%
Ohio	1,301.3	1,411.2	1,657.5	1,721.7	1,684.8	29%
Oklahoma	96.2	107.2	177.5	270.6	278.9	190%
Oregon	231.9	248.2	303.8	339.0	340.3	47%
Pennsylvania	1,107.7	1,167.4	1,413.9	1,425.0	1,377.3	24%

State	1999	2000	2005	2009	2010	Percent Change 1999-2010
Puerto Rico	166.0	182.8	258.4	325.2	339.2	104%
Rhode Island	44.3	48.4	55.4	60.9	62.3	41%
South Carolina	173.8	188.2	236.2	244.5	248.0	43%
South Dakota	38.3	43.5	58.5	73.0	76.4	99%
Tennessee	224.2	248.2	414.9	530.7	531.0	137%
Texas	802.9	964.9	1,781.3	2,676.1	2,831.5	253%
Utah	107.3	118.1	148.7	169.2	173.2	61%
Vermont	34.9	38.7	44.5	47.4	46.6	33%
Virgin Islands	6.1	7.5	8.5	9.4	8.9	46%
Virginia	312.8	347.8	519.0	588.1	585.9	87%
Washington	515.9	548.7	609.1	643.7	637.9	24%
West Virginia	109.4	120.3	171.1	187.5	204.6	87%
Wisconsin	532.5	569.0	601.2	611.3	602.3	13%
Wyoming	38.5	41.9	51.2	60.4	60.5	57%
Total	$15,901.2	$17,854.3	$23,005.9	$26,385.6	$26,555.7	67%

Source: Table prepared by the Congressional Research Service based on data from the Department of Health and Human Services, Office of Child Support Enforcement.

Table A-4.Trend in TANF/Foster Care Collections, by State,
FY1999-FY2009
(in millions of dollars)

State	1999	2000	2005	2009	Percent Change 1999-2009
Alabama	$18.0	$12.3	$11.8	$13.9	-23%
Alaska	17.6	16.9	15.3	13.7	-22%
Arizona	23.3	26.4	30.3	26.3	13%
Arkansas	10.8	10.1	6.9	8.2	-25%
California	620.2	750.7	611.9	493.5	-20%
Colorado	31.9	30.2	21.3	18.4	-42%
Connecticut	54.1	50.0	44.9	41.5	-23%
Delaware	7.4	7.2	6.1	6.4	-14%
District of Columbia	5.1	4.5	6.0	7.9	56%
Florida	73.1	75.2	71.8	62.3	-15%
Georgia	47.8	43.8	39.1	30.2	-37%
Guam	1.6	1.4	1.3	2.4	51%
Hawaii	10.4	11.7	10.5	11.5	11%
Idaho	4.1	4.3	3.7	3.8	-8%
Illinois	72.8	81.3	36.8	36.5	-50%
Indiana	25.2	24.2	31.9	29.5	17%
Iowa	44.1	43.7	37.4	34.2	-22%
Kansas	28.9	28.2	21.9	23.7	-18%
Kentucky	35.9	33.5	34.9	38.7	8%
Louisiana	17.8	16.4	14.3	15.1	-15%
Maine	32.6	34.0	29.0	27.6	-15%
Maryland	25.1	25.3	20.5	21.8	-13%
Massachusetts	54.2	46.7	41.1	44.6	-18%
Michigan	129.1	130.0	95.5	102.9	-20%
Minnesota	60.7	56.7	49.8	40.9	-33%
Mississippi	11.0	8.3	7.2	7.3	-33%
Missouri	37.0	46.8	40.8	44.0	19%

State	1999	2000	2005	2009	Percent Change 1999-2009
Montana	6.1	5.7	4.9	4.7	-24%
Nebraska	12.9	12.0	10.4	9.0	-30%
Nevada	7.4	8.4	7.3	8.7	17%
New Hampshire	8.6	9.5	8.7	7.2	-16%
New Jersey	72.5	65.7	59.4	58.5	-19%
New Mexico	10.8	7.9	9.2	9.0	-16%
New York	182.0	193.1	121.7	111.3	-39%
North Carolina	44.0	44.9	36.3	26.8	-39%
North Dakota	4.8	4.3	6.2	5.6	16%
Ohio	93.9	99.5	69.9	80.9	-14%
Oklahoma	20.5	20.0	18.5	18.2	-11%
Oregon	23.8	22.9	23.7	28.0	18%
Pennsylvania	97.4	95.3	102.8	72.0	-26%
Puerto Rico	2.1	2.7	2.0	2.1	-2%
Rhode Island	18.1	17.0	11.6	6.8	-62%
South Carolina	15.4	13.4	10.9	17.0	11%
South Dakota	13.7	16.4	3.9	3.1	-77%
Tennessee	30.1	31.3	65.8	57.0	89%
Texas	108.2	82.4	82.7	64.2	-41%
Utah	20.4	19.2	17.2	12.5	-39%
Vermont	8.4	8.8	5.4	4.3	-49%
Virgin Islands	0.5	0.8	0.2	0.3	-41%
Virginia	37.8	36.4	45.4	41.6	10%
Washington	95.2	92.7	77.9	71.6	-25%
West Virginia	5.8	16.1	13.5	10.5	81%
Wisconsin	37.7	43.2	31.0	30.6	-19%
Wyoming	3.7	3.4	2.7	2.6	-30%
Total	$2,481.7	$2,593.1	$2,191.1	$1,970.8	-21%

Source: Table prepared by the Congressional Research Service based on data from the Department of Health and Human Services, Office of Child Support Enforcement.

Table A-5. Trend in Non-TANF Collections, by State, FY1999-FY2009
(in millions of dollars)

State	1999	2000	2005	2009	Percent Change 1999-2009
Alabama	$167.9	$179.8	$225.5	$252.1	50%
Alaska	49.6	54.2	69.8	82.9	67%
Arizona	145.9	170.4	236.3	288.5	98%
Arkansas	97.7	110.4	148.2	193.9	98%
California	984.0	1,308.8	1,610.2	1,651.8	68%
Colorado	131.7	145.9	214.9	262.9	100%
Connecticut	121.4	140.9	190.5	211.7	74%
Delaware	37.5	41.8	60.4	67.2	79%
District of Columbia	30.1	30.5	41.9	44.7	49%
Florida	506.7	572.8	1,004.9	1,227.0	142%
Georgia	282.9	318.1	459.8	558.8	98%
Guam	6.0	6.3	7.6	10.0	67%
Hawaii	50.2	54.8	73.1	87.0	73%
Idaho	60.2	70.8	111.8	137.2	128%
Illinois	252.7	279.9	525.0	760.3	201%
Indiana	245.9	342.0	449.4	574.8	134%
Iowa	157.1	175.0	252.6	294.3	87%
Kansas	109.1	111.0	130.7	157.5	44%
Kentucky	170.4	192.9	301.7	354.9	108%
Louisiana	170.3	197.5	275.0	324.4	90%
Maine	48.0	55.4	71.7	76.0	58%
Maryland	325.0	342.6	432.9	467.8	44%
Massachusetts	237.3	271.9	425.0	502.4	112%
Michigan	1,145.6	1,217.4	1,286.0	1,289.0	13%
Minnesota	381.9	420.7	519.1	557.2	46%
Mississippi	117.9	136.1	188.2	246.5	109%
Missouri	248.9	292.2	426.7	510.4	105%
Montana	32.1	35.0	41.9	49.7	55%
Nebraska	97.7	130.5	148.8	179.8	84%
Nevada	84.7	70.9	108.2	145.3	72%
New Hampshire	57.6	61.9	72.1	75.1	30%
New Jersey	562.6	613.5	856.1	1,016.7	81%
New Mexico	24.1	31.7	59.2	83.2	245%
New York	727.8	908.9	1,278.4	1,511.3	108%
North Carolina	304.0	350.7	528.9	628.4	107%
North Dakota	36.1	37.6	56.8	73.5	104%
Ohio	1,207.5	1,311.7	1,587.6	1,640.8	36%
Oklahoma	75.7	87.2	159.0	252.4	233%

State	1999	2000	2005	2009	Percent Change 1999-2009
Oregon	208.1	225.3	280.1	311.0	49%
Pennsylvania	1,010.3	1,072.1	1,311.1	1,353.0	34%
Puerto Rico	163.9	180.1	256.4	323.1	97%
Rhode Island	26.2	31.4	43.7	54.1	106%
South Carolina	158.4	174.8	225.3	227.4	44%
South Dakota	24.6	27.1	54.6	69.9	184%
Tennessee	194.1	216.9	349.1	474.4	144%
Texas	694.7	882.5	1,698.6	2,611.9	276%
Utah	86.9	98.9	131.5	156.6	80%
Vermont	26.5	29.9	39.1	43.1	63%
Virgin Islands	5.7	6.7	8.3	9.1	59%
Virginia	275.0	311.4	473.6	546.5	99%
Washington	420.7	456.0	531.2	572.1	36%
West Virginia	103.6	104.2	157.6	177.1	71%
Wisconsin	494.8	525.8	570.2	580.6	17%
Wyoming	34.7	38.5	48.6	57.8	67%
Total	$13,419.5	$15,261.2	$20,814.8	$24,414.8	82%

Source: Table prepared by the Congressional Research Service based on data from the Department of Health and Human Services, Office of Child Support Enforcement.

Table A-6. Average Monthly Child Support Payments in Cases with Collections, by State, FY1999-FY2009

State	1999	2000	2005	2009	Percent Change 1999-2009
Alabama	$147	$149	$164	$167	14%
Alaska	204	209	216	259	27%
Arizona	183	193	218	232	27%
Arkansas	135	145	169	202	49%
California	174	215	237	246	41%
Colorado	163	191	361	213	30%
Connecticut	194	199	221	220	13%
Delaware	145	150	200	211	45%
District of Columbia	181	187	214	213	18%
Florida	170	177	210	231	36%
Georgia	138	165	196	223	61%
Guam	199	191	95	240	21%
Hawaii	198	198	316	275	39%
Idaho	188	158	189	196	4%
Illinois	167	172	215	257	54%
Indiana	173	216	244	259	50%
Iowa	172	155	172	187	9%

Table A-6. (Continued)

State	1999	2000	2005	2009	Percent Change 1999-2009
Kansas	254	181	181	193	-24%
Kentucky	165	168	188	191	16%
Louisiana	144	156	184	205	42%
Maine	169	180	208	219	30%
Maryland	203	212	247	263	29%
Massachusetts	246	256	333	337	37%
Michigan	197	236	272	259	32%
Minnesota	267	273	298	308	15%
Mississippi	120	125	142	157	31%
Missouri	164	181	214	214	31%
Montana	138	141	152	170	23%
Nebraska	216	215	208	221	2%
Nevada	271	185	201	221	-18%
New Hampshire	212	225	256	265	25%
New Jersey	249	259	329	378	52%
New Mexico	144	170	206	235	63%
New York	189	208	256	285	51%
North Carolina	187	149	175	195	4%
North Dakota	215	184	220	259	20%
Ohio	497	270	260	255	-49%
Oklahoma	245	143	178	210	-14%
Oregon	180	186	222	235	30%
Pennsylvania	234	245	279	312	33%
Puerto Rico	161	165	198	220	37%
Rhode Island	188	199	223	223	19%
South Carolina	162	168	196	198	22%
South Dakota	863	170	197	224	-74%
Tennessee	158	169	206	216	37%
Texas	266	265	240	289	8%
Utah	173	177	209	231	33%
Vermont	192	202	222	254	33%
Virgin Islands	N.A.	N.A.	178	144	N.A.
Virginia	153	159	202	223	45%
Washington	200	201	206	210	5%
West Virginia	177	192	213	216	22%
Wisconsin	217	212	223	228	5%
Wyoming	179	176	179	203	14%
Total	$201	$206	$231	$246	22%

Source: Table prepared by the Congressional Research Service based on data from the Department of Health and Human Services, Office of Child Support Enforcement.
Note: N.A.—Not Available.

Table A-7. Collections on Behalf of TANF Families as a Percentage of Total CSE Collections, by State, FY1999-FY2009

State	1999	2000	2005	2009
Alabama	10%	6%	5%	5%
Alaska	26%	24%	18%	14%
Arizona	14%	13%	11%	8%
Arkansas	10%	8%	4%	4%
California	39%	36%	28%	23%
Colorado	20%	17%	9%	7%
Connecticut	31%	26%	19%	16%
Delaware	16%	15%	9%	9%
District of Columbia	15%	13%	13%	15%
Florida	13%	12%	7%	5%
Georgia	14%	12%	8%	5%
Guam	21%	18%	15%	19%
Hawaii	17%	18%	13%	12%
Idaho	6%	6%	3%	3%
Illinois	22%	23%	7%	5%
Indiana	9%	7%	7%	5%
Iowa	22%	20%	13%	10%
Kansas	21%	20%	14%	13%
Kentucky	17%	15%	10%	10%
Louisiana	9%	8%	5%	4%
Maine	40%	38%	29%	27%
Maryland	7%	7%	5%	4%
Massachusetts	19%	15%	9%	8%
Michigan	10%	10%	7%	7%
Minnesota	14%	12%	9%	7%
Mississippi	9%	6%	4%	3%
Missouri	13%	14%	9%	8%
Montana	16%	14%	10%	9%
Nebraska	12%	8%	7%	5%
Nevada	8%	11%	6%	6%
New Hampshire	13%	13%	11%	9%
New Jersey	11%	10%	6%	5%
New Mexico	31%	20%	13%	10%
New York	20%	18%	9%	7%
North Carolina	13%	11%	6%	4%
North Dakota	12%	10%	10%	7%
Ohio	7%	7%	4%	5%
Oklahoma	21%	19%	10%	7%
Oregon	10%	9%	8%	8%
Pennsylvania	9%	8%	7%	5%

Table A-7. (Continued)

State	1999	2000	2005	2009
Puerto Rico	1%	1%	1%	1%
Rhode Island	41%	35%	21%	11%
South Carolina	9%	7%	5%	7%
South Dakota	36%	38%	7%	4%
Tennessee	13%	13%	16%	11%
Texas	13%	9%	5%	2%
Utah	19%	16%	12%	7%
Vermont	24%	23%	12%	9%
Virgin Islands	8%	11%	2%	3%
Virginia	12%	10%	9%	7%
Washington	18%	17%	13%	11%
West Virginia	5%	13%	8%	6%
Wisconsin	7%	8%	5%	5%
Wyoming	10%	8%	5%	4%
Total	16%	15%	10%	7%

Source: Table prepared by the Congressional Research Service based on data from the Department of Health and Human Services, Office of Child Support Enforcement.

Table A-8. Trend in Total CSE Expenditures, by State, FY1999-FY2010 (in millions of dollars)

State	1999	2000	2005	2009	2010	Percent Change 1999-2010
Alabama	$53.5	$57.1	$61.2	$68.4	$ 69.0	29%
Alaska	18.0	21.5	21.3	24.4	25.6	42%
Arizona	58.7	60.6	64.2	72.1	63.9	9%
Arkansas	36.8	40.5	46.3	48.6	62.0	68%
California	612.7	676.0	1,084.7	1,067.8	943.3	54%
Colorado	52.0	63.1	72.8	68.9	75.4	45%
Connecticut	38.6	55.4	69.0	75.0	72.5	88%
Delaware	18.2	18.7	24.2	29.5	25.3	39%
District of Columbia	13.2	16.0	22.5	29.5	27.1	105%
Florida	190.5	216.3	252.6	293.7	291.9	53%
Georgia	89.9	110.4	107.9	90.6	101.7	13%
Guam	3.8	3.2	4.5	4.6	4.9	28%
Hawaii	20.1	16.4	20.4	22.2	23.2	15%
Idaho	10.5	19.7	22.6	31.3	25.9	147%
Illinois	138.8	158.7	165.4	189.0	192.2	38%
Indiana	38.5	50.5	57.9	78.9	82.0	113%
Iowa	42.6	54.6	52.5	61.4	56.0	31%

State	1999	2000	2005	2009	2010	Percent Change 1999-2010
Kansas	49.6	51.2	50.8	59.2	58.9	19%
Kentucky	56.2	59.7	59.6	54.8	60.5	8%
Louisiana	47.3	46.5	65.5	78.1	79.9	69%
Maine	18.6	19.9	24.8	28.3	28.1	51%
Maryland	82.7	109.8	99.7	109.4	145.8	76%
Massachusetts	75.1	95.7	82.5	81.3	120.9	61%
Michigan	164.5	246.9	211.5	242.1	205.0	25%
Minnesota	113.1	120.2	139.6	166.3	163.2	44%
Mississippi	30.6	31.4	24.1	30.5	48.5	59%
Missouri	94.4	106.6	90.8	92.9	88.0	-7%
Montana	11.6	13.4	13.5	14.3	14.9	29%
Nebraska	32.0	38.3	47.3	41.5	41.9	31%
Nevada	38.0	41.1	47.3	47.1	64.8	71%
New Hampshire	16.9	16.0	18.3	19.5	21.1	25%
New Jersey	139.1	157.0	203.9	293.5	262.0	88%
New Mexico	32.3	33.6	36.5	50.6	43.8	36%
New York	212.8	239.9	313.3	372.7	372.8	75%
North Carolina	130.1	111.6	119.9	135.0	131.4	1%
North Dakota	10.0	9.7	11.4	14.9	16.1	61%
Ohio	274.4	302.0	301.3	355.9	263.8	-4%
Oklahoma	32.3	42.6	51.4	71.1	75.2	133%
Oregon	42.3	49.5	55.5	66.6	69.0	63%
Pennsylvania	183.5	199.4	228.8	246.9	251.3	37%
Puerto Rico	29.8	30.1	45.1	42.7	35.0	17%
Rhode Island	10.9	11.8	9.2	8.3	20.2	85%
South Carolina	36.7	39.3	35.1	53.0	54.0	47%
South Dakota	6.6	7.1	8.3	9.4	7.4	11%
Tennessee	52.2	55.8	82.4	75.4	84.7	62%
Texas	202.9	207.4	283.0	287.0	336.8	66%
Utah	36.3	37.0	39.6	45.5	43.9	21%
Vermont	9.0	10.3	12.1	14.2	14.5	61%
Virgin Islands	2.6	5.3	4.8	5.8	7.5	190%
Virginia	75.7	79.4	87.7	89.7	93.8	24%
Washington	118.1	129.4	136.7	148.5	153.2	30%
West Virginia	28.7	31.2	37.2	40.4	43.2	50%
Wisconsin	96.7	90.1	115.2	92.3	107.4	11%
Wyoming	8.8	10.7	9.0	9.9	5.4	-39%
Total	$4,039.0	$4,525.8	$5,352.6	$5,850.3	$5,775.6	43%

Source: Table prepared by the Congressional Research Service based on data from the Department of Health and Human Services, Office of Child Support Enforcement.

APPENDIX B. DISTRIBUTION OF CHILD SUPPORT PAYMENTS AND THE "FAMILY FIRST POLICY"

Child support collections are distributed to families or retained by governments as reimbursement for welfare costs. Nonwelfare collections go to families. Welfare collections can be split among the federal and state governments, with some payments to families. Under P.L. 104-193, the rules governing how child support collections are distributed among families, the federal government, and state governments changed substantially. Pursuant to P.L. 109-171, effective October 1, 2008, at state option, the child support distribution rules were changed again.

Since the CSE program's inception, the rules determining who actually gets the child support arrearage payments have been complex. It is helpful to think of the rules in two categories. First, there are rules in both federal and state law that stipulate who has a legal claim on the payments owed by the noncustodial parent. These are called assignment rules. Second, there are rules that determine the order in which child support collections are paid in accord with the assignment rules. These are called distribution rules.

Many analysts and commentators were concerned that the distribution rules that were enacted as part of the 1996 welfare reform law (P.L. 104-193) were difficult for states to follow, for staff to explain, for parents to understand, and for computers to implement. They generally agreed that the rules created accounting nightmares for customers, litigation from advocacy groups, headaches for computer programmers, and audit deficiencies for the states.[51]

According to one CSE director, child support distribution rules became extremely complex once a family leaves welfare:

> Most of the problems stem from the requirements that pre-assistance arrears be assigned to the state, and that certain arrearages otherwise owed to the former welfare family are deemed to be owed to the state when the collection is made by federal tax refund intercept.
>
> When a family leaves welfare, states are required to keep track of six categories of arrearages: permanently assigned, temporarily assigned, conditionally assigned, never assigned, unassigned during assistance, and unassigned pre-assistance. On the computer, these different categories are called "buckets." The money shifts among the buckets according to the source of the collection, the family's status on or off assistance when the arrearage accrued, the amount of the unreimbursed public assistance balance, and the date of the assignment of support rights as well as the date the TANF

case closed (because of phased-in implementation dates). Moreover, the distribution rules differ, depending on whether the family went on welfare before or after October 1, 1997.[52]

Much of the complexity of the distribution rules stemmed from their gradual implementation and federal/state receipt of child support arrearage payments collected through the federal income tax refund offset program. Thus, some of the complexity of the rules ended when the rules were completely implemented on October 1, 2000. Many observers contend that if states choose to implement the "family first" approach authorized by P.L. 109-171, the distribution of child support will be much easier to explain, understand, and carry out.

Current TANF Recipients

As a condition of TANF eligibility, when a family applies for TANF, the custodial parent must assign to the state the right to collect both current child support payments and past-due child support obligations that accrue while the family is on the TANF rolls (these are called permanently-assigned arrearages[53]). The assignment requirement for TANF applicants also includes arrearage payments that accumulated *before* the family enrolled in TANF (these are called pre-assistance arrearages).

While the family receives TANF benefits, the state is permitted to retain any current support and any assigned arrearages it collects *up to the cumulative amount of TANF benefits that have been paid to the family.* P.L. 104-193 repealed the $50 required pass through[54] and gave states the choice to decide how much, if any, of the state share (some, all, none) of child support payments collected on behalf of TANF families to send the family. States also decide whether to treat child support payments as income to the family. P.L. 104-193 required states to pay the federal government the federal government's share of TANF collections.

P.L. 109-171 stipulated that the assignment covers child support that accrues *only* during the period that the family receives TANF. Thus, child support owed before a family enrolls in TANF and after the family leaves TANF belongs to the family, and child support owed during the time the family is on TANF belongs to the state and federal governments. This provision took effect on October 1, 2009, or October 1, 2008, at state option.[55]

For families who receive assistance from the state, P.L. 109-171 required the federal government to waive its share of the child support collections passed through to TANF families by the state and disregarded by the state—up to an amount equal to $100 per month in the case of a family with one child, and up to $200 per month in the case of a family with two or more children. This provision took effect on October 1, 2008.

Former TANF Recipients

Before 1996, once a family went off AFDC, child support arrearage payments generally were divided between the state and federal governments to reimburse them for AFDC; if any money remained, it was given to the family. In contrast, under P.L. 104-193, payments to families that leave AFDC/TANF are more generous. Under P.L. 104-193, arrearages are to be paid to the family first, unless they are collected from the federal income tax refund (in which case, reimbursing the federal and state governments is to be given first priority).

For Collections Made on or Since October 1, 2000

If a custodial parent assigns her or his child support rights to the state on or after October 1, 2000, the parent has to assign all support rights that accrue while the family is receiving TANF benefits. In addition, the TANF applicant must temporarily assign to the state all rights to support that accrued to the family before it began receiving TANF benefits. This temporary assignment lasts until the family stops receiving TANF benefits.

This means that since October 1, 2000, states have been required to distribute to former TANF families the following child support collections first before the state and the federal government are reimbursed: (1) all current child support, (2) any child support arrearages that accrue *after* the family leaves TANF (these arrearages are called never-assigned arrearages), plus any arrearages that accrued *before* the family began receiving TANF benefits. As mentioned above, these rules do not apply to child support collections obtained by intercepting federal income tax refunds. If child support arrearages are collected via the federal income tax refund offset program, the 1996 law stipulates that the state and federal government are to retain those collections.

The result of the 1996 welfare reform law distribution changes is that states are required to pay a higher fraction of child support collections on arrearages to families that have left welfare by making these payments to families first (before any payments are made to the state and the federal government). If this change in policy resulted in states losing money relative to previous law (as in effect in FY1995), the federal government was required to reimburse states for any losses (i.e., the "hold harmless" provision). This hold harmless provision (included in P.L. 106-169) was repealed, effective October 1, 2001. (The hold harmless provision was in effect from FY1998-FY2001.)

For Collections Made On or After October 1, 2009, or October 1, 2008, at State Option

P.L. 109-171 (the Deficit Reduction Act of 2005) simplified child support distribution rules to give states the option of providing families that have left TANF the full amount of the child support collected on their behalf (i.e., both current child support and child support arrearages, including support payments collected via the federal income tax refund offset program). The federal government will have to share with the states the costs of paying child support arrearages to the family first. This provision took effect on October 1, 2009, or October 1, 2008, at state option.

2011 GAO Report

According to a GAO report published in 2011:

> Most states nationwide have not implemented "family first" policy options since DRA. Several state CSE officials GAO interviewed said they support "family first" policies in principle, but funding constraints prevented implementing these options, because giving more child support collections to families means states retain less as reimbursement for public assistance costs.[56]

End Notes

[1] P.L. 104-193, the Personal Responsibility and Work Opportunity Reconciliation Act of 1996, ended Aid to Families with Dependent Children (AFDC) and related programs, replacing them with a "block grant" program of Temporary Assistance for Needy Families (TANF). States were required to end their AFDC programs and begin TANF by July 1, 1997. Most states opted to begin their TANF program sooner.

[2] U.S. Congress, Senate Committee on Finance, *Social Services Amendments of 1974*, report to accompany H.R. 17045, 93rd Cong. 2nd sess., S.Rept. 93-1356, p. 42.

[3] Families who receive TANF cash benefits, Medicaid benefits, or whose children receive Title IV-E foster care payments automatically are enrolled (free of charge) in the CSE program. Other families must apply for CSE services, and states must charge an application fee that cannot exceed $25. In addition, states have the option of recovering costs in excess of the application fee. Such recovery may be from either the custodial parent or the noncustodial parent.

[4] States were historically required to provide CSE services to Indian tribes and tribal organizations as part of their CSE caseloads. The 1996 welfare reform law (P.L. 104-193) allowed direct federal funding of tribal CSE programs at a 90% federal matching rate. In FY2010, 38 Indian tribes or tribal organizations operated comprehensive tribal CSE programs and nine Indian tribes or tribal organizations operated start-up tribal CSE programs. (For additional information, see CRS Report R41204, *Child Support Enforcement: Tribal Programs*, by Carmen Solomon-Fears.)

[5] There are three exceptions to the immediate income withholding rule: (1) if one of the parties demonstrates, and the court (or administrative process) finds that there is good cause not to require immediate withholding, (2) if both parties agree in writing to an alternative arrangement, or (3) at the HHS Secretary's discretion, if a state can demonstrate that the rule will not increase the effectiveness or efficiency of the state's CSE program.

[6] The CSE program has reciprocating agreements regarding the enforcement of child support with 15 countries: Australia, Canada (10 provinces/territories), Czech Republic, El Salvador, Finland, Hungary, Ireland, Israel, Netherlands, Norway, Poland, Portugal, Slovak Republic, Switzerland, and the United Kingdom of Great Britain and Northern Ireland.

[7] The Federal Parent Locator Service (FPLS) is a service operated by OCSE to help state CSE agencies locate parents in order to obtain child support payments. The FPLS obtains address and employer information from federal agencies. The FPLS also includes the Federal Child Support Case Registry and the National Directory of New Hires.

[8] P.L. 104-193, the 1996 welfare reform law, required states, beginning October 1, 1997, to establish an automated directory of new hires containing information from employers (including federal, state, and local governments and labor organizations) for each newly hired employee, that includes the name, address and Social Security number of the employee and the employer's name, address, and tax identification number. Within three business days after receipt of new hire information from the employer, the State Directory of New Hires is required to submit its new hire reports to the National Directory of New Hires. Contrary to its name, the National Directory of New Hires includes more than just information on new employees. It is a database that includes information on (1) all newly hired employees, compiled from state reports (and reports from federal employers), (2) the wage reports of existing employees, and (3) unemployment insurance claims. For additional information, see CRS Report RS22889, *The National Directory of New Hires*, by Carmen Solomon-Fears.

[9] There are three exceptions to the immediate income withholding rule: (1) if one of the parties demonstrates, and the court (or administrative process) finds that there is good cause not to require immediate withholding, (2) if both parties agree in writing to an alternative arrangement, or (3) at the HHS Secretary's discretion, if a state can demonstrate that the rule will not increase the effectiveness or efficiency of the state's CSE program.

[10] Before this DRA provision became effective in FY2008, the federal government was required to match (at the 66% rate) incentive funds that states reinvested in the CSE program. P.L. 111-5, the American Recovery and Reinvestment Act of 2009, temporarily reinstated federal matching of incentive payments for FY2009 and FY2010. There is currently no federal match on incentive payments.

[11] P.L. 109-171 required families who have never been on the TANF program to pay a $25 annual user fee when the CSE program collects at least $500 in child support annually (from the noncustodial parent) on their behalf. P.L. 109-171 provides the state with four options on how to collect the fee. The $25 user fee may be (1) retained by the state from

child support collected on behalf of the family (but the $25 cannot be part of the first $500 collected in any given federal fiscal year); (2) paid by the custodial parent; (3) recovered/recouped from the noncustodial parent; or (4) paid by the state out of state funds. (If the $25 annual user fee is paid by the state out of state funds, it is not considered an administrative cost of the CSE program and thus is not eligible for 66federal matching % funds.)

[12] See CRS Report R40946, *The Temporary Assistance for Needy Families Block Grant: An Introduction*, by Gene Falk.

[13] In 1984, Congress reinstated authority for the state CSE agencies to take steps (when appropriate) to secure an assignment to the state for any rights to support on behalf of Title IV-E foster care children and to collect child support on behalf of those children. This authority had been inadvertently deleted in 1980 when the foster care program was transferred from Title IV-A of the Social Security Act to Title IV-E of the Social Security Act. Child support collected on behalf of such foster care children is retained by the state as reimbursement for foster care maintenance payments with appropriate reimbursement to the federal government. The public agency responsible for supervising the placement of the child may use the collection in excess of the foster care payment in the manner it determines will best serve the interests of the child, including setting such payments aside for the child's future needs or making all or a part of the payments available to the person responsible for meeting the child's day-to-day needs. Child support paid in excess of amounts ordered to meet the child's need may be retained by the state to reimburse it and the federal government for any past foster care maintenance payments or AFDC/TANF payments made with respect to the child. The data in the tables and figures in this report generally include child support payments collected on behalf of foster care children, unless otherwise noted. Likewise, the caseload numbers also include Title IV-E foster care children who are being served by the CSE program. In FY2003, CSE collections made on behalf of foster care cases amounted to less than 0.4% of total CSE collections; OCSE does not collect data specifically on foster care cases.

[14] As mentioned below, a mother with two children by different fathers would be considered two families or cases by the CSE program and one family or case by the TANF program. Thereby, the 2.2 million CSE cases receiving TANF cash assistance differ from the 2.0 million TANF cases.

[15] As mentioned earlier, the AFDC program was replaced with the TANF block grant pursuant to P.L. 104-193, which was enacted August 22, 1996.

[16] Under the old jargon, former TANF families would have been included among non-TANF families.

[17] In FY2004, families currently receiving TANF comprised almost 17% of the CSE caseload and received 5% of CSE collections (see **Table A-7**). In contrast, former TANF families comprised 46% of the CSE caseload and received 43% of CSE collections. Families that have never been on TANF comprised 37% of the CSE caseload and also received 43% of CSE collections. In FY2004, the state data reporting forms were revised to include information on child support collected for Medicaid reimbursement on behalf of families that had never been on TANF. These collections totaled $1.9 billion in FY2004, almost 9% of CSE collections.

[18] Local programs may receive additional funding from either the state or local government, or both, pursuant to the state's CSE plan.

[19] In FY2010, 92% of CSE collections ($24.5 billion) went to the families on the CSE rolls.

[20] Before FY2007, the federal government reimbursed states at a higher 90% matching rate for the laboratory costs associated with establishing paternity. Pursuant to P.L. 109-171, the higher federal matching rate for laboratory costs of paternity testing was reduced to the general federal CSE reimbursement rate of 66% beginning October 1, 2006.

[21] The 1996 welfare reform law (P.L. 104-193) repealed a previous requirement that $50 be passed through to the family, and gave states the choice to decide how much, if any, of the

state share (some, all, none) of child support payments collected on behalf of TANF families to send the family. States also decide whether to treat child support payments as income to the family. Moreover, P.L. 104-193 required states to pay the federal government the federal government's share of TANF collections. (As of August 2004, 21 states were, on a monthly basis, providing a pass through and disregard up to $50—higher in a couple of states—of child support collected on behalf of TANF families.)

[22] Under pre-1996 law, a small percentage of AFDC collections was paid to the family as a result of the $50 "pass through" payment, or in cases when the child support payment exceeded the AFDC benefit. Under old law, the first $50 of current monthly child support payments collected on behalf of an AFDC family was given to the family and disregarded as income to the family so that it did not affect the family's AFDC eligibility or benefit status. P.L. 104- 193 repealed the $50 disregard/pass through provision.

[23] A lower administrative cost figure for a state may result in a greater federal incentive payment by improving the state's collections-to-costs ratio.

[24] Other CSE financing changes made pursuant to P.L. 109-171 include provisions that (1) reduce the CSE federal matching rate for the laboratory costs associated with establishing paternity from 90% to 66% and (2) eliminate the federal match on CSE incentive payments that states, in compliance with federal law, reinvest back into the CSE program.

[25] Medical child support is the legal provision of payment of medical, dental, prescription, and other health care expenses of dependent children. It can include provisions to cover health insurance costs as well as cash payments for unreimbursed medical expenses. According to CSE data, more than 90% of medical child support is provided in the form of health insurance coverage. The requirement for medical child support is a part of all child support orders (administered by CSE agencies), and it only pertains to the parent's dependent children. Activities undertaken by CSE agencies to establish and enforce medical child support are eligible for federal reimbursement at the CSE matching rate of 66%. To the extent that medical support is assigned to the state, medical support collections are forwarded to the Medicaid agency; otherwise, the amount is paid to the family.

[26] It was recognized that the "family first" policy also would reduce the amount of child support that states and the federal government would be able to keep. To protect states from losses expected to result from this new "family first" policy, Congress included a "hold harmless" provision in the 1996 welfare reform law (P.L. 104-193), ensuring that if states did not reach their FY1995 level of child support collections, the federal government would make up the difference. One result of the hold harmless provision is that it also helped states affected by declining welfare collections caused by a drop in the TANF caseload. The hold harmless grant came out of the federal share of CSE collections attributable to that state (i.e., the same source of funding as the incentive payment). Some observers argued successfully that the hold harmless provision was not sustainable. They noted that at some point, the federal share of child support collections would be depleted by the incentive payments and the hold harmless awards. They maintained that when this occurred, money would have to be found elsewhere to finance the hold harmless payment, and that it was unlikely that Congress would provide states with the additional funding when the federal government was already paying 66% of CSE expenditures. P.L. 106-169 (enacted November 18, 1999) limited the hold harmless requirement in FY2000 and FY2001, and repealed the hold harmless provision, effective October 1, 2001 (FY2002).

[27] See http://www.acf.hhs.gov/programs/cse/pubs/2004/Strategic_Plan_FY2005-2009.pdf.

[28] P.L. 109-171 gives states the option of distributing to former TANF families the full amount of child support collected on their behalf (i.e., both current support and all child support arrearages—including arrearages collected through the federal income tax refund offset program). Thereby, P.L. 109-171 allows states to simplify the CSE distribution process by eliminating the special treatment of child support arrearages collected through the federal income tax refund offset program.

[29] National Governor's Association, *HR-14: Child Support Financing*, Winter Meeting, 1999.

[30] Note that in current dollars (i.e., not adjusted for inflation), total CSE collections dropped for the first time in its history in FY2009. In current dollars, total CSE collections increased 0.6% between FY2009 and FY2010.

[31] U.S. Department of Health and Human Services, *Office of Child Support Enforcement FY 2009 Preliminary Report*, May 2010, p. 1. **Note:** OCSE data indicate that during the period FY2008-FY2010, child support collections from income withholding (the most used method of enforcing child support payments) dropped by 2%, from 68% in FY2008 to 66.5% in FY2010; and child support collections via the unemployment compensation offset increased by 235%, from 2% of collections in FY2008 to 6.7% of collections in FY2010.

[32] The federal "loss" was computed by summing the gross federal share of administration, actual incentive payments, and hold harmless payments and then subtracting the gross federal share of child support collections. The financial "gain" to states was computed by subtracting from total administrative expenses the federal share of administrative expenses, actual incentive payments, hold harmless payments, and the state share of child support collections. Differences in methodologies might yield different "loss" and "gain" figures.

[33] General Accounting Office, *Child Support Enforcement: Effects of Declining Welfare Caseloads Are Beginning to Emerge*, GAO/HEHS-99-105, June 1999, p. 2.

[34] The federal medical assistance percentage (FMAP), which determines the federal share of CSE collections made on behalf of TANF and foster care families, has a statutorily set maximum and minimum rate. The maximum federal matching rate for child support is 83% and the minimum federal matching rate for child support is 50%. The reader should note that in the past the FMAP generally was referred to as the Medicaid matching rate.

[35] Although AFDC was replaced by the TANF block grant pursuant to P.L. 104-193 (enacted August 22, 1996), the same matching rate (i.e., FMAP) procedure is still used.

[36] Levin Group, Inc. and ECONorthwest, *State Financing of Child Support Enforcement Programs*, November 23, 1998.

[37] The 1996 welfare law prohibits use of TANF funds for a family that includes a person who has not assigned support rights to the state, and it requires states to cut a family's TANF benefit by at least 25% if a recipient does not cooperate with child support rules (and may expel the family from TANF).

[38] Under the old incentive payment system, each state received a minimum incentive payment equal to at least 6% of the state's total amount of child support collections made on behalf of AFDC/TANF families for the year, plus at least 6% of the state's total amount of child support collections made on behalf of non-AFDC/TANF families for the year. The amount of a state's incentive payment could reach a maximum of 10% of the AFDC/TANF collections, plus 10% of the non-AFDC/TANF collections, depending on the state's ratio of CSE collections to CSE expenditures. There was a limit (i.e., cap), however, on the incentive payment for non-AFDC/TANF collections. The incentive payment for such collections could not exceed 115% of incentive payments for AFDC/TANF collections.

[39] P.L. 105-200 stipulated that the aggregate incentive payment to the states could not exceed the following amounts: $422 million for FY2000, $429 million for FY2001, $450 million for FY2002, $461 million for FY2003, $454 million for FY2004, $446 million for FY2005, $458 million for FY2006, $471 million for FY2007, and $483 million for FY2008. For the years after FY2008, the aggregate incentive payment to the states is to be increased to account for inflation.

[40] In FY1998, the incentive payment, which at that point in time came out of the gross federal share of child support collected on behalf of TANF families, was $395 million. Beginning in FY2002, child support incentive payments were no longer paid out of the federal share of child support collections made on behalf of TANF families. Instead, federal funds have been specifically appropriated out of the U.S. Treasury for CSE incentive payments.

[41] Under the old incentive payment system, HHS made incentive payments to states for their child support enforcement systems, based solely on one factor: cost-effectiveness.

[42] A 2003 report commissioned by HHS indicated that for the nation as a whole, federal CSE incentive payments to states represented 25% of CSE financing for the states (in aggregate). Source: State Financing of Child Support Enforcement Programs: Final Report, prepared for the Assistant Secretary for Planning and Evaluation and the Office of Child Support Enforcement, Department of Health and Human Services, prepared by Michael E. Fishman, Kristin Dybdal of the Lewin Group, Inc. and John Tapogna of ECONorthwest, September 3, 2003, p. iii.

[43] Some observers also contend that there are intangible benefits (such as personal responsibility and parental involvement) associated with the collection of child support that should be taken into account in determining the merits of the CSE program. This discussion does not address the intangible benefit concept.

[44] Urban Institute, prepared for the Department of Health and Human Services, Administration for Children and Families, Office of Child Support Enforcement, *Child Support Cost Avoidance in 1999, Final Report*, by Laura Wheaton, June 6, 2003, Contract No. 105-00-8303 http://www.acf.hhs.gov/programs/cse/pubs/2003/reports/ cost_avoidance/#N100E7.

[45] The CSE program is estimated to handle 50%-60% of all child support cases; the remaining cases are handled by private attorneys, collection agencies, or through mutual agreements between the parents.

[46] Center for Law and Social Policy, *Families Will Lose At Least $8.4 Billion in Uncollected Child Support If Congress Cuts Funds—and Could Lose Billions More*, by Vicki Turetsky, updated January 18, 2006, p. 4.

[47] Center on Budget and Policy Priorities, *Unshared Sacrifice: Who's Hurt, Who's Helped, and What's Spared under the Emerging House Budget Reconciliation Plan*, by Sharon Parrott and Isaac Shapiro, November 2, 2005 http://www.cbpp.org/10-28-05bud.htm.

[48] U.S. Government Accountability Office, *Child Support Enforcement: Departures from Long-term Trends in Sources of collections and Caseloads Reflect Recent Economic Conditions*, GAO-11-196, January 2011, pp. 20-21.

[49] As noted earlier, P.L. 111-5 temporarily reinstated the federal match on incentive payments for FY2009 and FY2010.

[50] The general CSE federal matching rate is 66%. This means that for every dollar that a state spends on its CSE program, the federal government will reimburse the state 66 cents. So if the state spends $1 on its program, the federal share of that expenditure is 66 cents and the state share of that expenditure is 34 cents. The algebraic formula for this relationship is represented by $.66/.34=x/1$. Thereby, if the state share of the expenditure is $1, the federal share is $1.94 (i.e., the federal share is 1.94 times the state share), and the total expenditure by the state is $2.94 ($1+$1.94). Similarly, if the state share of expenditures amounted solely to the incentive payment of $504 million, the federal share would amount to 1.94 times that amount, or $978 million, translating into $1.482 billion in CSE expenditures/funding.

[51] *More Money for Former Welfare Moms: Simplify the Distribution Rules*, by Marilyn Ray Smith, presented at a Congressional seminar for the House Committee on Ways and Means sponsored by the American Enterprise Institute and the Brookings Institution, October 22, 1999, p. 5.

[52] Ibid., pp. 3-4.

[53] This is one of the following six categories of arrearages: (1) permanently-assigned arrearages, (2) temporarily- assigned arrearages, (3) conditionally-assigned arrearages, (4) never-assigned arrearages, (5) unassigned during- assistance arrearages, and (6) unassigned pre-assistance arrearages. The six categories are defined in OCSE Transmittal 97-17, October 21, 1997, *Instructions for the distribution of child support under Section 457 of the Social Security Act*, http://www.acf.dhhs.gov/programs/cse/pol/AT/at-9717.htm, p. 6.

[54] Under prior law, a small percentage of AFDC collections was paid to the family as a result of the $50 "pass through" payment or in cases when the child support payment exceeded the AFDC benefit. Under old law, the first $50 of current monthly child support payments

collected on behalf of an AFDC family was given to the family and disregarded as income to the family so that it did not affect the family's AFDC eligibility or benefit status.

[55] P.L. 109-171 gives states the option to discontinue pre-assistance arrearage assignments in effect on September 30, 1997, or pre-assistance arrearage assignments in effect after September 30, 1997, and before the implementation date of this provision. If a state chooses to discontinue the child support arrearage assignment, the state would have to give up its legal claim to collections based on such arrearages, and the state would have to distribute the collections to the family.

[56] U.S. Government Accountability Office, *Child Support Enforcement: Departures from Long-Term Trends in Sources of Collections and Caseloads Reflect Recent Economic Conditions*, GAO-11-196, January 2011, p. Highlights.

In: Child Support Enforcement Program   ISBN: 978-1-62808-384-2
Editor: Pascal Chollet   © 2013 Nova Science Publishers, Inc.

Chapter 3

CHILD SUPPORT ENFORCEMENT PROGRAM INCENTIVE PAYMENTS: BACKGROUND AND POLICY ISSUES*

Carmen Solomon-Fears

SUMMARY

The Child Support Enforcement (CSE) program, enacted in 1975, to help strengthen families by securing financial support from noncustodial parents, is funded with both state and federal dollars. The federal government bears the majority of CSE program expenditures and provides incentive payments to the states (which include Washington, DC, and the territories of Guam, Puerto Rico, and the Virgin Islands) for success in meeting CSE program goals. In FY2011, total CSE program expenditures amounted to $5.7 billion. The aggregate incentive payment amount to states was $513 million in FY2011.

P.L. 105-200, the Child Support Performance and Incentive Act of 1998, established a revised incentive payment system that provides incentive payments to states based on a percentage of the state's CSE collections and incorporates five performance measures related to establishment of paternity and child support orders, collections of current and past-due support payments, and cost-effectiveness. P.L. 105-200 set specific annual caps on total federal

---

* This is an edited, reformatted and augmented version of the Congressional Research Service Publication, CRS Report for Congress RL34203, dated May 2, 2013.

incentive payments and required states to reinvest incentive payments back into the CSE program. The exact amount of a state's incentive payment depends on its level of performance (or the rate of improvement over the previous year) when compared with other states. In addition, states are required to meet data quality standards. If states do not meet specified performance measures and data quality standards, they face federal financial penalties.

P.L. 109-171 (the Deficit Reduction Act of 2005) prohibited federal matching (effective October 1, 2007, i.e., FY2008) of state expenditure of federal CSE incentive payments. However, in 2009 P.L. 111-5 (the American Recovery and Reinvestment Act of 2009) required the Department of Health and Human Services (HHS) to temporarily provide federal matching funds (in FY2009 and FY2010) on CSE incentive payments that states reinvested back into the CSE program. Thus (since FY2011), CSE incentive payments that are received by states and reinvested in the CSE program are no longer eligible for federal reimbursement. The FY2008 repeal of federal reimbursement for incentive payments reinvested in the CSE program garnered much concern over its fiscal impact on the states and renewed interest in the incentive payment system per se.

A comparison of FY2002 incentive payment performance score data to FY2011 performance score data shows that CSE program performance has improved with respect to all five performance measures. Although CSE incentive payments were awarded to all 54 jurisdictions in FY2002, FY2005, FY2010, and FY2011 (the years covered in this report), some jurisdictions performed poorly on one or more of the five performance measures. Even so, on the basis of the unaudited FY2011 performance incentive scores of the 54 jurisdictions, 53 jurisdictions received an incentive for all five performance measures, and 1 jurisdiction (the Virgin Islands) received an incentive for four performance measures.

Despite a general consensus that the CSE program is doing well, questions still arise about whether the program is effectively meeting its mission and concerns exist over whether the program will be able to meet future expectations. Several factors may cause a state not to receive an incentive payment that is commensurate with its relative performance on individual measures. These factors include static or declining CSE collections; sliding scale performance scores that financially benefit states at the upper end (but not the top) of the artificial threshold and financially disadvantaged states at the lower end of the artificial threshold; a limited number of performance indicators that do not encompass all of the components critical to a successful

CSE program; and a statutory maximum on the aggregate amount of incentive payments that can be paid to states. These factors are discussed in the context of the following policy questions: (1) Does the CSE incentive payment system reward good performance? (2) Should incentive payments be based on additional performance indicators? (3) Should Temporary Assistance for Needy Families (TANF) funds be reduced because of poor CSE performance? (4) Why aren't the incentives and penalties consistent for the paternity establishment performance measure? (5) Should incentive payments be based on individual state performance rather than aggregate state performance? and (6) Will the elimination of the federal match of incentive payments adversely affect CSE programs?

INTRODUCTION

Since the Child Support Enforcement (CSE) program's enactment in 1975, the federal government has paid incentives (monetary payments) to states to encourage them to operate efficient and effective CSE programs.[1] The incentive payment system is part of the CSE program's strategic plan that rewards states for working to achieve the goals and objectives of the program. Incentive payments, although small when compared to federal reimbursement payments for state and local CSE activities, are a very important component of the CSE financing structure. Together with the incentive payment system is a penalty system that imposes financial penalties on states that fail to meet certain performance levels. The purpose of the two complementary systems is to reward states for results while holding them accountable for poor performance, thereby motivating states to focus their efforts on providing vital CSE services.

Before FY2008, the federal government was required to match incentive funds that states reinvested in the CSE program, at a federal matching rate of 66%. P.L. 109-171 (the Deficit Reduction Act of 2005) prohibits federal matching (effective October 1, 2007) of state expenditure of federal CSE incentive payments.[2] This means that CSE incentive payments that are received by states and reinvested in the CSE program are no longer eligible for federal reimbursement. The repeal of federal matching funds for incentive payments reinvested in the CSE program garnered much concern over its fiscal impact on the states and renewed interest in the incentive payment system per se. Given the loss of that funding source and the resulting cost shift to the states (during a time when many interests are competing for limited state dollars), attention has focused on the individual elements of the performance-based incentive payment system and whether they need to be modified to ensure that the CSE program remains effective and efficient.

This report describes the current CSE incentive payment system, provides information on financial penalties that are imposed on states if incentive payment data are unreliable or if performance standards are not met, explains how state incentive payments are derived, discusses some of the state trends, and presents some policy issues concerning incentive payments.

In addition, the report includes two appendices. **Appendix A** presents a legislative history of CSE incentive payments. **Appendix B** includes several detailed state tables that display unaudited incentive performance scores for each of the five performance measures.[3] **Table B-1** shows the amount of incentive payments received by states for FY2002, FY2005, FY2010, and FY2011. **Table B-2** displays unaudited incentive performance scores for each of the five performance measures for FY2002. **Table B-3** displays unaudited incentive performance scores for each of the five performance measures for FY2005. **Table B- 4** displays unaudited incentive performance scores for each of the five performance measures for FY2010.

Table B-5 displays unaudited incentive performance scores for each of the five performance measures for FY2011.

BACKGROUND

The CSE program was enacted in 1975 as a federal-state-local partnership. It helps strengthen families by securing financial support from noncustodial parents. The CSE program serves both welfare and non- welfare families. In FY2011, the CSE program collected $27.3 billion in child support payments and served 15.8 million child support cases. In FY2011, total CSE program expenditures amounted to $5.7 billion, of which $513 million were incentive payments (i.e., 9% of total program expenditures). In FY2011, the CSE program collected $5.12 in child support (from noncustodial parents) for every dollar spent on the program. The CSE program is funded with both state and federal dollars. The federal government bears the majority of CSE program expenditures and provides incentive payments to the states for success in meeting CSE program goals.[4]

Financing Elements of the CSE Program

There are five funding streams for the CSE program.

First, states spend their own money to operate a CSE program; the level of funding allocated by the state and localities determines the amount of total resources available to CSE agencies.

Second, the federal government reimburses each state 66% of all allowable expenditures on CSE activities. The federal government's funding is "open-ended" in that it pays its percentage of expenditures by matching the amounts spent by state and local governments with no upper limit or ceiling. The federal government's financial participation in the CSE program is the program's largest revenue source.

Third, the federal government provides states with an incentive payment to encourage them to operate effective programs.[5] Federal law requires states to reinvest CSE incentive payments back into the CSE program or related activities. Effective October 1, 2007, P.L. 109-171 (enacted February 8, 2006) prohibited federal matching of state expenditures of federal CSE incentive payments. However, in 2009 P.L. 111-5 required HHS to temporarily provide federal matching funds (in FY2009 and FY2010) on CSE incentive payments that states reinvest back into the CSE program. Thus, starting again in FY2011, CSE incentive payments that are received by states and reinvested in the CSE program are no longer eligible for federal reimbursement.

Fourth, states collect child support on behalf of families receiving Temporary Assistance for Needy Families (TANF) to reimburse themselves (and the federal government) for the cost of TANF cash payments to the family. Federal law requires families who receive TANF cash assistance to assign their child support rights to the state in order to receive TANF. In addition, such families must cooperate with the state if necessary to establish paternity and secure child support. CSE collections on behalf of families receiving TANF cash benefits are used to reimburse state and federal governments for TANF payments made to the family (i.e., child support payments go to the state instead of the family, except for amounts that states choose to "pass through" to the family as additional income that does not affect TANF eligibility or benefit amounts).

The formula for distributing the child support payments collected by the states on behalf of TANF families between the state and the federal government is still based on the old Aid to Families with Dependent Children (AFDC) federal-state reimbursement rates,[6] even though the AFDC entitlement program was replaced by the TANF block grant program.[7] Under existing law, states have the option of giving some, all, or none of their share of child support payments collected on behalf of TANF families to the family. Pursuant to P.L. 109-171 (effective October 1, 2008), states that choose to pass through some of the collected child support to the TANF family do not have to pay the federal government their shares of such collections if the amount passed through to the family and disregarded by the state does not exceed $100 per month ($200 per month for a family with two or more children) in child support collected on behalf of a TANF (or foster care) family.

Fifth, application fees and costs recovered from nonwelfare families help finance the CSE program. In the case of nonwelfare families, the custodial parent can hire a private attorney or apply for CSE services on their own. The CSE agency must charge an application fee, not to exceed $25, for families not on welfare who apply for CSE services. The CSE agency may charge this fee to the applicant or the noncustodial parent, or pay the fee out of state funds. In addition, a state may at its option recover costs in excess of the application fee. Such recovery may be either from the custodial parent or the noncustodial parent. Fees and costs recovered from nonwelfare cases must be subtracted from the state's total administrative costs before calculating the federal reimbursement amount (i.e., the 66% matching rate).

Moreover, effective October 1, 2006, P.L. 109-171 requires families that have never been on TANF to pay a $25 annual user fee when child support enforcement efforts on their behalf are successful (i.e., at least $500 annually is collected on their behalf). The state can collect the user fee from the custodial parent, the noncustodial parent, or the state can pay the fee out of state funds. This annual user fee is separate from the application fee.[8]

Cap on Incentive Payments

As mentioned earlier, from the outset incentive payments were provided by the federal government to the states to encourage them to operate effective CSE programs. The 1996 welfare reform law (P.L. 104-193) required the Secretary of the Department of Health and Human Services (HHS), in consultation with state CSE directors, to develop and recommend to Congress a new incentive payment system that was revenue neutral. A report on CSE Incentive Funding was presented to Congress in February 1997.

P.L. 105-200, the Child Support Performance and Incentive Act of 1998 (enacted July 16, 1998), replaced the old incentive payment system to states[9] with a revised revenue-neutral (with respect to the federal government) incentive payment system that (1) provided incentive payments based on a percentage of the state's CSE collections; (2) incorporated five performance measures related to establishment of paternity and child support orders, collections of current and past-due child support payments, and cost-effectiveness; (3) phased in the incentive system, with it being fully effective beginning in FY2002; (4) required reinvestment of incentive payments into the CSE program; and (5) used an incentive payment formula weighted in favor of TANF and former TANF families.[10]

The requirement that the new incentive payment system be revenue neutral resulted in an annual cap on incentive payments. Congress capped incentive payments by legislating the total amount of incentive payments that states (in aggregate) could earn in each fiscal year. Federal law stipulated that the aggregate incentive payment to the states could not exceed the following amounts: $422 million for FY2000, $429 million for FY2001, $450 million for FY2002, $461 million for FY2003, $454 million for FY2004, $446 million for FY2005, $458 million for FY2006, $471 million for FY2007, and $483 million for FY2008. Since FY2008, the aggregate incentive payment to the states has been increased to account for inflation.[11] Congress based the capped aggregate incentive payment amount on Congressional Budget Office (CBO) projections of incentive payments at the time that the Child Support Performance and Incentive bill was passed.[12]

Purpose of the Current CSE Incentive Payment System

P.L. 105-200, the Child Support Performance and Incentive Act of 1998, revised the original incentive payment system in an effort to further improve the CSE program by linking incentive payments to states' performance in five major areas. Instead of rewarding states only for their program's cost-effectiveness, the revised incentive payment system was designed to reward states for good performance in five different areas that were closely related to children obtaining child support payments (from their noncustodial parent). The revised incentive payment system was touted as one that would provide real incentives for the states to improve the CSE program, help families attain self-sufficiency, and support important societal goals like paternity identification and parental responsibility.[13]

P.L. 105-200 also revised the financial penalty system for the CSE program to reflect that improved performance is especially critical in three areas: paternity establishment, child support order establishment, and current child support collections. If specified performance standards are not met in these three areas, financial penalties through a reduction in the state's TANF block grant are imposed.

The revised/current CSE incentive payment system added an element of uncertainty to what used to be a somewhat predictable source of income for states. Although in the aggregate, states receive higher incentive payments than under the earlier incentive payment system, the total amount available is fixed (as noted in the previous section), and individual states have to compete with each other for their share of the capped funds. Under the revised incentive system, whether or not a state receives an incentive payment for good performance and the total amount of its incentive payment depends on several factors: the total amount of money available in a given fiscal year from which to make incentive payments, the state's success in obtaining collections on behalf of its caseload,[14] the state's performance in five areas (see text box below), the reliability of a state's data, and the relative success or failure of other states in making collections and meeting the performance criteria.

Moreover, unlike the old incentive system which allowed states and counties to spend incentive payments on whatever they chose, the current incentive payment system requires that the incentive payment be reinvested by the state into either the CSE program or some other activity which might lead to improving the efficiency or effectiveness of the CSE program (e.g., mediation/conflict-resolution services to parents, parenting classes, efforts to improve the earning capacity of noncustodial parents, etc.). Also, federal matching funds are no longer available to increase the value of incentive payments.

CALCULATION OF STATE CSE INCENTIVE PAYMENTS

The CSE incentive payment structure is very complex. For a fuller explanation of how state incentive payments are calculated, see the example given in the CSE FY2011 preliminary report.[15]

CSE incentive payments to states are based on several factors including state collections of child support payments and the performance of the states in five areas. The five performance measures are related to (1) establishment of paternity, (2) establishment of child support orders, (3) collection of current child support, (4) collection of child support arrearages (i.e., past-due child support), and (5) cost-effectiveness of the CSE program.

CSE PERFORMANCE MEASURES

(1) *Paternity Establishment.* States have two options:
   (A) CSE Paternity Establishment Percentage (PEP). State performance on paternity establishment is calculated by dividing the total number of children in the state's CSE caseload during the fiscal year (or at state option at the end of the fiscal year) who were born outside of marriage and for whom paternity has been established by the total number of children in the state's CSE caseload as of the end of the preceding fiscal year who were born outside of marriage;
   (B) Statewide Paternity Establishment Percentage (PEP). State performance on paternity establishment is calculated by dividing the total number of minor children who were born outside of marriage and for whom paternity has been established during the fiscal year by the total number of children born outside of marriage during the preceding fiscal year.

(2) *Establishment of Child Support Orders.* State performance on support orders is calculated by dividing the number of cases in the CSE caseload for which there is a support order by the total number of cases in the program.

(3) *Current Payments.* State performance on current payments is obtained by dividing the total dollars collected for current support in cases in the CSE caseload by the total amount owed on support in these cases which is not past-due.

(4) *Arrearage Payments.* State performance on arrears (i.e., past-due payments) is obtained by dividing the number of cases in which there was some payment on arrearages during the fiscal year by the total number of cases in which past-due support is owed. (Cases in which the family was formerly on welfare, and in which arrearages are collected by federal income tax intercept, do not count as an arrearage payment case unless the state shares the collection with the family.)

(5) *Cost-Effectiveness.* State performance on cost-effectiveness is determined by dividing the total amount collected through the child support program by the total amount spent by the program to make these collections.

Under the CSE incentive payment system, each of the five performance measures is translated into a mathematical formula (see text box that follows). The amount of incentive payments for a particular performance measure is based on a standard that is specified in law. For each performance standard, there is an upper threshold. All states that achieve performance levels at or above this upper threshold are entitled to the maximum possible incentive for that performance measure. Simultaneously, there is also a minimum level of performance below which states do not receive an incentive, unless the state makes significant improvement over its previous year's performance.

To determine a state's incentive payment, the following computations must be made. First, each state's performance percentage for each performance measure is separately determined and translated into the applicable percentage for that particular performance measure. If the performance percentage is at or above the upper threshold, the applicable percentage for that performance measure would be 100%. If the performance percentage is below the lower threshold, the applicable percentage for that performance measure would be 0%.[16] If the performance percentage is in between these two points (the upper and lower thresholds), the applicable percentage is obtained by referring to the tables specified in federal law (Section 458(b)(6) of the Social Security Act) for each of the performance measures. For example, with regard to the establishment of child support orders, if the state's performance percentage for this measure is 70%, meaning that 70% of CSE cases in the state have a child support order, the applicable percentage is 80%.

Second, after the applicable percentage for each performance measure is determined, that percentage is multiplied by the "collections" base for an individual state. The collections base is calculated by using the following formula: [2 x (current assistance collections + former assistance collections + Medicaid never assistance collections)+ never on TANF collections + fees retained by other states].[17]

Performance Thresholds (and applicable percentage)

If PEP	≥ 80%, then 100%	if < 50%, then 0%
If order establishment	≥ 80%, then 100%	if < 50%, then 0%
If current support	≥ 80%, then 100%	if < 40%, then 0%
If arrearages	≥ 80%, then 100%	if < 40%, then 0%
If cost-effectiveness	≥ 5.00, then 100%	if < 2.00, then 0%

Third, if the performance measure is paternity establishment, child support order establishment, or current collections, then the resulting amount (i.e., the applicable percentage multiplied by the collections base) is multiplied by 100%. If the performance measure is past-due collections (i.e., arrearages) or cost- effectiveness, then the resulting amount is multiplied by 75%. These calculations result in maximum incentives for each performance measure.

Fourth, the maximum incentives are added together. The dollar amount that is obtained by adding together the five maximum incentives for each performance measure is called the maximum incentive base amount.

Fifth, all of the states' (includes the four jurisdictions: the District of Columbia, Guam, Puerto Rico, and the Virgin Islands) maximum incentive base amounts are then added together for a total maximum incentive base amount.

Sixth, each state's individual maximum base amount is compared to the total maximum incentive base amount. The mathematical formula would be— maximum state incentive base/sum of all state incentive bases. An individual state's share of the total is the percentage that is used to determine the state's actual incentive payment. For example, if a state's share of the total is 17%, then the state will receive 17% of the capped incentive payment for the fiscal year in question. In FY2011 for example, the state's incentive payment would be $87,210,000 (.17* $513 million).

The federal government makes incentive payments to states on an on-going quarterly prospective basis using state *estimates* of what their incentive payments will total. After the audited performance data (discussed below) are available, OCSE reconciles the incentive payment actually earned with the amount previously estimated, and received, by the state.[18]

Data Reliability

Before enactment of P.L. 105-200, incentive payments (under the old system) were not dependent on data reliability. Although audits were performed at least once every three years to ensure compliance with federal CSE program requirements, the audits were focused on administrative procedures and processes rather than performance outcomes and results.

Under current federal law, states are accountable for providing reliable data on a timely basis or they receive no incentive payments. The data reliability provisions were enacted as part of P.L. 105-200, which established the current incentive payment system. They are in the law to ensure the integrity of the incentive payment system. The federal Office of Child Support Enforcement (OCSE) Office of Audit performs data reliability audits to evaluate the completeness, accuracy, security, and reliability of data reported and produced by state reporting systems. The audits help ensure that incentives under the Child Support Performance and Incentives Act of 1998 (P.L. 105-200) are earned and paid only on the basis of verifiable data and that the incentive payments system is fair and equitable. If an audit determines that a state's data are not complete and reliable for a given performance measure, the state receives zero payments for that measure[19] and are subject to federal financial penalties. Although estimated incentive payments are sent to states on a prospective quarterly basis, those estimated incentive payments are reconciled to the actual incentive payment earned after the auditing process. Thus, if a state fails the audit on a particular performance measure, the state would not receive an incentive payment for that measure (i.e., the state's funding would be reduced to reflect the audit's findings).[20]

The audit for the fiscal year generally begins at the beginning of a calendar year (after the fiscal year has ended) and is completed by early summer.[21] States provide the assigned regional OCSE office with a universe of cases and audit trails. From this universe, a sample is selected. The auditor selects at least 150 cases from the state's universe. States are required to provide auditors with documentation, through access to state computerized/automated systems and hard copies of documents for each of the sample cases. The auditor reviews the sample cases to determine if the items he or she is trying to verify are correct. For example, if the documentation indicates that $450 in current support was paid during the fiscal year, the auditor looks up the collection history for that particular case on the state's automated system to determine if the $450 figure is correct. Federal regulations (Title 45 CFR Section 305.1(i)) require data to meet a 95% standard of reliability.[22] Once the audit is completed, the general practice is for an auditor from a different field office to review the findings. Moreover, the OCSE headquarters staff that work on audits also review audit findings. Informational sessions and opportunities to contest the findings are available to states during the audit process.[23]

FEDERAL FINANCIAL PENALTIES

The CSE performance-based penalty system provides that a financial penalty be assessed when data submitted for calculating state performance are found to be incomplete or unreliable. Penalties may also be assessed when the calculated level of performance for any of three performance measures—paternity establishment, support order establishment, or current collections—fails to achieve a specified level or when states are not in compliance with certain child support requirements.

There is an automatic corrective action year if performance measures and data reliability are not achieved. The corrective action year is the immediately succeeding fiscal year following the year of the deficiency. If the state's data are determined complete and reliable and the related performance is adequate for the corrective action year, the penalty is not imposed.

If the corrective action was unsuccessful, the financial penalty is a reduction in the state's TANF block grant. Historically, Congress has linked the CSE program and the TANF (and old AFDC) program. Currently Section 402(a)(2) of the Social Security Act (Title IV-A which deals with TANF (and used to pertain to the AFDC program)) stipulates that the governor of a state must certify that it will operate an approved CSE program as a condition of receiving TANF block grant funding. Since the enactment of the CSE program in 1975, there has always been a provision in federal law that linked poor performance (and penalties) or noncompliance in the CSE program with a reduction in Title IV-A funding.

Under the performance-based audit procedures (Section 409(a)(8) of the Social Security Act), a graduated penalty equal to 1%-5% of the federal TANF block grant is assessed against a state if (1) on the basis of the data submitted by the state for a review, the state CSE program fails to achieve the paternity establishment or other performance standards set by the HHS Secretary;[24] (2) an audit finds that the state data are incomplete or unreliable; or (3) the state failed to substantially comply with one or more CSE state plan requirements, and the state fails to correct the deficiencies in the fiscal year following the performance year (i.e., the corrective action plan year).

The penalty amount is calculated as not less than 1% nor more than 2% of the TANF block grant program for the first year of the deficiency. The penalty amount increases each year, up to 5%,[25] for each consecutive year the state's data are found to be incomplete, unreliable, or the state's performance on a penalty measure fails to attain the specified level of performance. According to the CSE annual data report for FY2010: "One state showed a deficiency related to the PEP and will have one corrective action year to correct the deficiency."[26]

STATE TRENDS

A state's share of incentive payments depends on many factors that are distinct to its population and CSE caseload. CSE collection can be straightforward. In most CSE cases paternity has already been established and in a majority of cases the child support order was established at the time of the divorce or separation. Further, many noncustodial parents are up-to-date in their child support payments and do not owe any past-due (arrearage) payments. However, in other cases meeting CSE performance measures can be more difficult. Although not exactly sequential, the CSE performance measures are very interdependent. A child support order cannot be established if paternity has not been legally determined. Child support payments cannot be collected or enforced unless a child support order has been established. Arrearage payments cannot be collected if current child support is not paid. States that have more cases that require services such as paternity establishment, child support order establishment, and payment of arrearages generally have a tougher time collecting child support than states that do not face such challenges.

In FY2011, the aggregate incentive payment amount was $513 million. Among the 50 states and the 4 jurisdictions of the District of Columbia, Guam, Puerto Rico, and the Virgin Islands, CSE incentive payments in FY2011 ranged from a high of $59.6 million in Texas to a low of $77,575 in the Virgin Islands.[27]

As mentioned earlier, incentive payments are a function of a state's collections base, which is largely dependent on population size. Thus, the aggregate amount of incentive dollars received by individual states is a poor indicator of a state's performance with respect to individual performance measures. As discussed in more detail later, incentive payments are not directly correlated with performance. In other words, even though a state may receive a high incentive payment, the state's performance on one or several individual performance measures may be very poor. This results because child support collections are the critical determinant of incentive payments to states. In fact, the top seven states with regard to collecting child support were the top seven states with regard to high incentive payments in both FY2002 and FY2011 (and throughout much of the period in between).[28]

Performance Incentive Scores

The data presented in this report are based on the unaudited incentive payment performance scores. These data are readily available each year when OCSE publishes its preliminary data report. Over the years, states have made significant improvement in the area of data reliability. According to the final report on FY2009 data, only three jurisdictions failed data reliability audits.

A comparison of FY2002 performance score data to FY2011 performance score data[29] shows that CSE program performance has improved with respect to all five performance measures. The following scores represent the total score for all 54 jurisdictions for each of the performance measures (referred to in this analysis as national averages). The national average for the paternity establishment score went from 73% (CSE program measure rather than statewide measure) in FY2002 to 99% in FY2011; the score for child support order establishment increased from 70% to 81%; the score for current child support collections increased from 58% to 62%; the score for child support arrearage cases increased from 60% to 62%; and the cost-effectiveness score increased from 4.13 to 5.12.

The following analysis examines the individual CSE performance measures for the years FY2002, FY2005, FY2010, and FY2011. It focuses on the median,[30] maximum, and minimum scores for all five performance measures. The median score sometimes better illustrates trends because unlike the mean (i.e., average) it is not affected by very high or very low scores.

Table 1. Child Support Enforcement Performance Incentive Scores: National Averages (Selected Years)

Performance Measures	FY 2002	FY 2005	FY 2010	FY 2011
CSE Paternity Establishment Percentage	72.62	87.57	97.26	98.96
Child Support Order Establishment Score	70.40	75.87	80.02	80.92
Current Child Support Collections Score	57.55	59.91	61.96	62.44
Child Support Arrearage Cases Score	59.56	60.04	61.98	62.17
Cost-Effectiveness Score	4.13	4.58	4.88	5.12

Source: U.S. Department of Health and Human Services, Office of Child Support Enforcement, Preliminary Data Reports for the Selected Years.

Paternity Establishment Percentage (PEP)

One of the goals of the CSE program has always been to establish paternity for those needing that service. In fact the official title of the program when it was enacted in 1975 and to this day is Child Support and Establishment of Paternity. The CSE program's strategic plan for FY2005-FY2009[31] reiterated this by indicating that goal #1 of the program is that all children have an established parentage and the program tries to achieve this goal by increasing the percentage of children with a legal relationship with their parents.

As mentioned earlier in the CSE performance measures text box, states have two options for determining the Paternity Establishment Percentage (PEP). They can use a PEP that is based on data that pertain solely to the CSE program or they can use a PEP that is based on data that pertain to the state population as a whole. In effect, the PEP compares paternities established during the fiscal year with the number of nonmarital births during the preceding fiscal year. This calculation permits scores to exceed 100%. A PEP of 100% or more generally means that the state has established paternity for more than just the newborns who were born outside of marriage in the specified year (i.e., the state has established paternity for many older children as well).[32]

The median PEP score among the 54 jurisdictions[33] with CSE programs was 86.64 in FY2002, 91.47 in FY2005, 94.69 in FY2010, and 97.32 in FY2011. The maximum PEP score was 130.75 in FY2002, it rose to 112.42 in FY2005, 118.29 in FY2010, and 126.33 in FY2011. The minimum PEP score started at 50.83 in FY2002, increased to 54.05 in FY2005 and to 81.26 in FY2010, and then dropped to 77.98 in FY2011.

According to the CSE FY2010 Annual Report:

> Feedback from the field continues to suggest that states are facing greater challenges to maintain the high performance levels. At the time the incentive/penalty structure began, states had a backlog of cases that enabled them to exceed the 90 percent performance level for PEP. However, with the maturation of the system and the declining birth rate, many states have reduced or even eliminated their backlog of cases for establishing paternity. Normal annual variations in performance (91 percent rate one year, 89 percent the next) can result in a substantial penalty without indicating operational or performance problems. While the number of states currently receiving a penalty is still low, we believe that, in the future, more and more states will find it difficult to achieve the current acceptable performance level

and will allocate a disproportionate amount of resources to this function in an attempt to stay out of penalty status.[34]

Child Support Order Establishment Percentage

Goal #2 in the FY2005-FY2009 Strategic Plan of the Child Support Enforcement Program is for all children in the CSE caseload to have child support orders. The second performance measure focuses on the percentage of CSE cases that have a child support order (i.e., a legally-binding document that requires the noncustodial parent to pay child support).

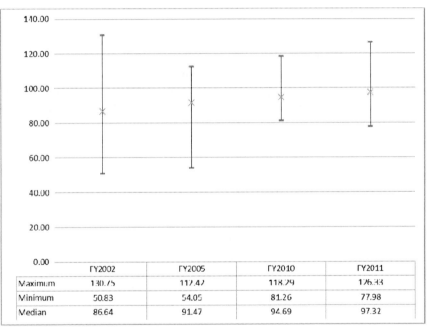

	FY2002	FY2005	FY2010	FY2011
Maximum	130.75	117.42	118.29	176.33
Minimum	50.83	54.05	81.26	77.98
Median	86.64	91.47	94.69	97.32

Source: Chart prepared by the Congressional Research Service based on data from the Office of Child Support Enforcement, Department of Health and Human Services.
Note: The x on the line graphs highlights the median score. In FY2002, on the basis of preliminary data, Guam had the maximum score (452.87). However, because of other conflicting data for Guam, that outlier PEP for Guam was excluded from this analysis. The next highest PEP score in FY2002 was 130.75 (Idaho).

Figure 1. Paternity Establishment Scores: Maximum, Median, Minimum (Selected Years).

The median child support order establishment score among the 54 jurisdictions with CSE programs rose in each of the years displayed, starting at 71.28 in FY2002 and ending at 82.90 in FY2011. The maximum score for this performance measure fluctuated; it started at 92.03 in FY2002, increased to 96.00 in FY2005, decreased to 92.38 in FY2010, and increased to 93.06 in FY2011. The minimum score for child support order establishment rose during the displayed years, starting at 29.66 in FY2002 and ending at 58.54 in FY2011.

Current Child Support Collections Scores

Goal #4[35] in the FY2005-FY2009 Strategic Plan of the Child Support Enforcement Program is for all children in the CSE caseload to receive the financial support owed by their noncustodial parents. This goal encompasses both current child support payments and past-due child support payments (i.e., arrearages). The third performance indicator measures the proportion of current child support owed that is collected on behalf of children in the CSE caseload.

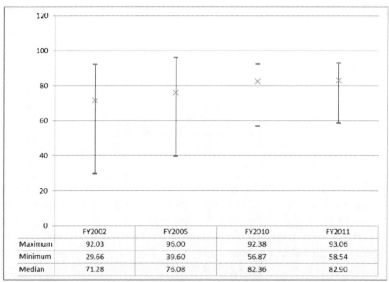

	FY2002	FY2005	FY2010	FY2011
Maximum	92.03	96.00	92.38	93.06
Minimum	29.66	39.60	56.87	58.54
Median	71.28	76.08	82.36	82.90

Source: Chart prepared by the Congressional Research Service based on data from the Office of Child Support Enforcement, Department of Health and Human Services.
Note: The x on the line graphs highlights the median score.

Figure 2. Child Support Order Establishment Scores: Maximum, Median, Minimum (Selected Years).

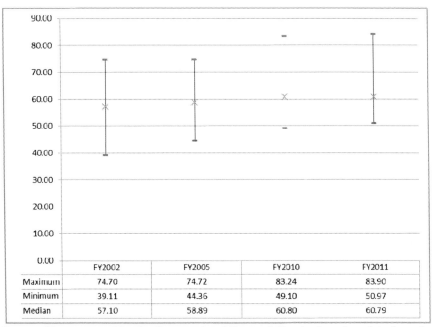

	FY2002	FY2005	FY2010	FY2011
Maximum	74.70	74.72	83.24	83.90
Minimum	39.11	44.36	49.10	50.97
Median	57.10	58.89	60.80	60.79

Source: Chart prepared by the Congressional Research Service based on data from the Office of Child Support Enforcement, Department of Health and Human Services.
Note: The x on the line graphs highlights the median score.

Figure 3. Child Support Current Collections Scores: Maximum, Median, Minimum (Selected Years).

The median child support current collections score among the 54 jurisdictions with CSE programs was 57.10 in FY2002, 58.89 in FY2005, 60.80 in FY2010, and remained relatively unchanged in FY2011 (60.79). The maximum score was 74.70 in FY2002 and 83.90 in FY2011. The minimum score increased from 39.11 in FY2002 to 50.97 in FY2011.

Child Support Arrearage Cases Scores

The fourth performance indicator measures state efforts to collect money from CSE cases with an arrearage (i.e., past-due child support payments are owed). This performance measure specifically counts paying cases—and not total arrearage dollars collected—because states have different methods of handling certain aspects of arrearage cases. For example, the ability to write off debt that is deemed uncollectible varies by state. Moreover, some states charge interest on arrearages (which is considered additional arrearages) while other states do not.[36] As mentioned above, this performance measure is incorporated in goal #4 as listed in the FY2005-FY2009 CSE Strategic Plan.

The median child support arrearage cases score among the 54 jurisdictions with CSE programs fluctuated during the years displayed. It was 60.71 in FY2002, 60.59 in FY2005, and 61.57 in both FY2010 and FY2011. The maximum score increased from 71.58 in FY2002 to 83.77 in FY2011. The minimum score rose from 30.21 in FY2002, increased to 45.61 in FY2010, and then declined to 45.37 in FY2011.

Cost-Effectiveness Scores

Goal #5 in the FY2005-FY2009 Strategic Plan of the Child Support Enforcement Program says that the CSE program will be efficient and responsive in its operations. The fifth performance measure assesses the total dollars collected by the CSE program for each dollar spent.

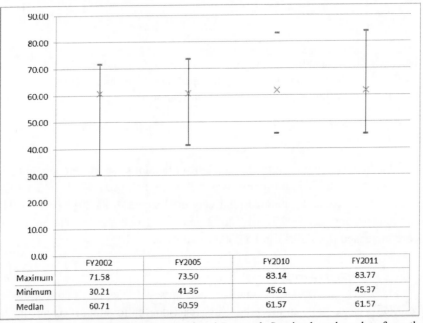

	FY2002	FY2005	FY2010	FY2011
Maximum	71.58	73.50	83.14	83.77
Minimum	30.21	41.36	45.61	45.37
Median	60.71	60.59	61.57	61.57

Source: Chart prepared by the Congressional Research Service based on data from the Office of Child Support Enforcement, Department of Health and Human Services.
Note: The x on the line graphs highlights the median score.

Figure 4. Child Support Arrearage Cases Scores: Maximum, Median, Minimum (Selected Years).

The median cost-effectiveness score among the 54 jurisdictions with CSE programs for the years displayed was 4.49 in FY2002, it rose to 4.77 in FY2005, then fell to 4.69 in FY2010, and increased to 5.30 in FY2011. The maximum score went from 7.80 in FY2002 to 12.54 in FY2010, and then dropped to 10.41 in FY2011. The minimum score was 1.46 in FY2002, reached 2.10 in FY2005, then dropped to 1.42 in FY2010, and increased to 1.98 in FY2011.

According to the CSE Annual Report for FY2010, "*Increases in this measure stem mainly from declines in state program expenditures due to funding shortfalls compared to collections that have not declined to the same extent, but have remained flat.*"[37]

Incentive Payments for All Performance Measures

Although CSE incentive payments were awarded to all 54 jurisdictions (including the 50 states, the District of Columbia, Guam, Puerto Rico, and the Virgin Islands) in FY2002, FY2005, FY2010, and FY2011, some jurisdictions performed poorly on certain performance measures and thereby did not receive an incentive for that measure. (See the earlier text box on performance thresholds for the percentage scores on each performance measure that do not warrant an incentive payment.) The 54 jurisdictions (in aggregate) improved their performance over the selected years. In FY2002, 46 jurisdictions received an incentive for all five performance measures compared to 53 jurisdictions in FY2005, FY2010, and FY2011.

On the basis of the unaudited FY2002 performance incentive scores of the 54 jurisdictions, 46 jurisdictions received an incentive for all five performance measures, 3 jurisdictions received an incentive for four performance measures (California, Hawaii, and Mississippi), and 5 jurisdictions (Illinois, New Mexico, the District of Columbia, Guam, and the Virgin Islands) received an incentive for three performance measures. (See **Table B-2**.)

On the basis of the unaudited FY2005 performance incentive scores of the 54 jurisdictions, 53 jurisdictions received an incentive for all five performance measures and the remaining jurisdiction (the District of Columbia) received an incentive for four performance measures. (See **Table B-3**.)

On the basis of the unaudited FY2010 performance incentive scores of the 54 jurisdictions, 53 jurisdictions received an incentive for all five performance measures, and 1 jurisdiction received an incentive for four performance measures (the Virgin Islands). (See **Table B-4**.)

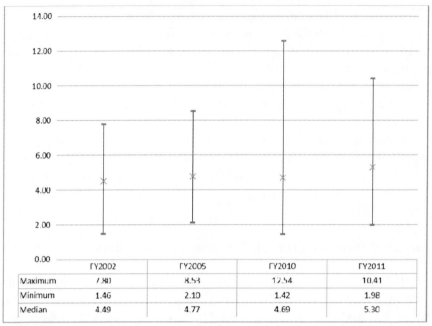

	FY2002	FY2005	FY2010	FY2011
Maximum	7.80	8.53	12.54	10.41
Minimum	1.46	2.10	1.42	1.98
Median	4.49	4.77	4.69	5.30

Source: Chart prepared by the Congressional Research Service based on data from the Office of Child Support Enforcement, Department of Health and Human Services.
Note: The x on the line graphs highlights the median score.

Figure 5. Cost-Effectiveness Scores: Maximum, Median, Minimum (Selected Years).

On the basis of the unaudited FY2011 performance incentive scores of the 54 jurisdictions, 53 jurisdictions received an incentive for all five performance measures, and 1 jurisdiction received an incentive for four performance measures (the Virgin Islands). (See **Table B-5.**)

Relationship between Incentive Payments and Performance Measures

Given that the incentive payment is based on five performance measures, it is likely that all jurisdictions would continue to receive some amount of incentive payments. However, if individual performance measures are examined, a different picture develops; some states may not perform well enough to receive an incentive payment with respect to one of the five performance measures. **Table B-2**, **Table B-3**, **Table B-4**, and **Table B-5** show the five performance measures by state (includes jurisdictions) for each of the four selected years (FY2002, FY2005, FY2010, and FY2011).[38] The states in each of the tables are ranked from highest performing state (relative to each indicator) to lowest performing state. These tables illustrate that the relationship between actual performance and CSE incentive payments is not always transparent. That is, even though a state may receive a high incentive payment, the state's performance on one or several individual performance measures may be very poor.

Child support collections are a very important component in determining the amount of a state's incentive payment. As mentioned earlier, incentive payments are a function of a state's collections base, which is composed of child support collected on behalf of current and former TANF families multiplied by two plus the collection amount made on behalf of families who have never been on TANF.[39] The main reason that there is not a more direct relationship between incentive payments and performance levels is that the incentive payment calculation is so heavily dependent on child support collections. The prominence of child support collections in the incentive payment formula results in the more populous states receiving the largest incentive payments.

Thus, a high collections base can mean that a state receives a high incentive payment despite low performance measures. For example, although California received the highest incentive payment in FY2002 and FY2005 and the second highest incentive payment in FY2010 and FY2011,[40] it ranked very low with regard to cost-effectiveness (51st in FY2002 and FY2005, 52nd in FY2010, and 51st in FY2011). However, because California collected substantially more child support payments than the next ranking state (21% more in FY2011) and because most of those collections were on behalf of TANF or former- TANF families (63% in FY2011), it is not surprising that California received the highest amount of incentive payments in FY2002 and FY2005 and the second highest amount in FY2010 and FY2011.[41] According to OCSE annual data reports, the top seven states with regard to collecting child support (in FY2002, FY2005, FY2010, and FY2011) were the top seven states with regard to high incentive payments (although not in the same rank order).

POLICY ISSUES

The current performance-based incentive payment system is part of the CSE program's strategic plan to set goals and measure results. Despite a general consensus that the CSE program is doing well, questions still arise about whether the program is effectively meeting its mission and concerns exist over whether the program will be able to meet future expectations in light of reductions in federal funding that were made pursuant to the Deficit Reduction Act of 2005 (P.L. 109-171).

Some in the CSE "community" (e.g., states, CSE workers, analysts, state policymakers, and advocates) contend that several factors may cause a state not to receive an incentive payment that is commensurate with its relative performance on individual measures. These factors include static or declining CSE collections; sliding scale performance scores that financially benefit states at the upper end (but not the top) of the artificial threshold and financially disadvantage states at the lower end of the artificial threshold; a limited number of performance indicators that do not encompass all of the components critical to a successful CSE program; and a statutory maximum on the aggregate amount of incentive payments that can be paid to states—which causes states to have to compete with each other for their share of the capped funds.

Others point out that the current CSE incentive payment system was developed with much thought and input from the CSE community. They maintain that the incentive payment formula rewards states for their performance in five critical areas, consistent with the legislated mission of the CSE program as well as the program's strategic plan and related outcome measures. They say that the performance thresholds were designed to provide tough but reachable targets for performance by rewarding states with higher incentives as they improve. In addition, it is argued that the annual cap on incentive payments (imposed by P.L. 105-200) has encouraged competition among the states and that there is no evidence that the cap has stifled the motivation of states to improve performance.

This section discusses the following list of issues: (1) "Does the CSE Incentive Payment System Reward Good Performance?" (2)"Should Incentive Payments Be Based on Additional Performance Indicators?" (3) "Should TANF Funds Be Reduced Because of Poor CSE Performance?" (4) "Why Aren't the Incentives and Penalties Consistent for the Paternity Establishment Performance Measure?" (5) "Should Incentive Payments Be Based on Individual State Performance Rather Than Aggregate State Performance?" and (6) "Will the Elimination of the Federal Match of Incentive Payments Adversely Affect CSE Programs?"

Does the CSE Incentive Payment System Reward Good Performance?

According to OCSE, all states received a CSE incentive payment in FY2011. This means that all states attained a certain level of program performance. According to OCSE, for all five performance measures, all states[42] achieved applicable percentage scores that earned them incentives. Moreover, a comparison of FY2002 data to FY2011 data shows that CSE program performance has improved for all five performance measures. The national average for the paternity establishment score increased from 73% (average of both the CSE measure and the statewide measure) in FY2002 to 98% in FY2011; the score for child support order establishment increased from 70% to 81%; the score for current child support collections increased from 58% to 62%; the score for child support arrearage cases increased from 60% to 62%; and the cost-effectiveness score increased from 4.13 to 5.12.

As discussed in the following sections, the design of the CSE incentive payment system raises questions about whether it is too heavily based on child support collections, and whether artificial thresholds adversely affect performance levels in that they unfairly allow states that are performing at significantly higher levels than other states to be given the same score (at the high end of the performance scale and at the low end of the performance scale).

CSE Collections

Ultimately the amount of a state's incentive payment depends on how much the state collects in child support payments. If a state has a small amount of child CSE collections, then even if it has high performance percentages for all five measures, its CSE incentive payment would be small.

Total child support collections for a state may vary for a number of reasons. Some factors that may influence the amount of child support a state collects include the population of the state, the number of single parents in the state, the number of children in the state, the number of unmarried parents in the state, the number of successful paternity determinations, the number of successful child support order establishments, the size of the TANF caseload, the size of the former-TANF caseload, the number of interstate cases, the effectiveness of the state's CSE program, state per capita income, state child poverty rate, and unemployment rate.

Artificial Thresholds Related to Performance Levels

All of the performance measures have a sliding scale so that increased performance earns a higher level of the incentive payment. However, they also all have upper and lower thresholds.[43] This means that above a certain percentage, all percentages are translated into the maximum applicable percentage. By the same policy, all performance percentages that are below a certain threshold percentage are translated into zero (i.e., the state would not be eligible for an incentive payment), unless the program improves sufficiently and quickly.

For performance measures pertaining to the establishment of paternity or the establishment of child support orders, if a state establishes paternity for at least 80% of its caseload or establishes a child support order for at least 80% of its caseload, the state receives a percentage score of 100%. In FY2011, this meant that Illinois, a state that established paternity for 84.95% of the children in the state without legally identified fathers, and Arizona, a state that established paternity for 126.33%[44] of the children in the state without legally identified fathers, both received a paternity establishment percentage score of 100%. (See **Table B-5.**) Thus, states separated by more than 40 percentage points received the same performance ranking—thereby not fully rewarding the performance of the more successful state. With regard to the establishment of child support orders, in FY2011, South Dakota, a state with an order establishment percentage of 93.06%, received the maximum possible percentage score of 100% as did Illinois, a state with a child support order establishment percentage of 80.13% (See **Table B-5.**)

By the same reasoning, the lower threshold of 50% treats states establishing zero paternities and zero child support orders the same as states establishing paternities or child support orders for 49% of their caseload. (In FY2011, no jurisdiction had an applicable percentage score below 50% for either paternity establishment or child support order establishment.)

The upper threshold for the current collections performance measure also is 80% but the lower threshold is 40%. The performance measure for current child support collections is based on the amount of collections (i.e., a dollar measure). In FY2011, one state (Pennsylvania, 83.90%) exceeded the upper threshold and thereby received a score of 100%. The other states had scores that were less than the upper threshold and more than the lower threshold. The lowest percentage attained was 51.11% (Nevada). (See **Table B-5.**)

Likewise, the upper threshold for the arrearage (i.e., past-due) collections performance measure is 80% and the lower threshold is 40%.[45] The performance measure for arrearage child support collections assesses the state's efforts to collect money from noncustodial parents for past-due support (i.e., a case ["person"] measure). In FY2011, one state (Pennslyvania, 83.77%) exceeded the upper threshold and thereby received a score of 100%. The other states had scores that were less than the upper threshold and more than the lower threshold. The lowest percentage attained was 45.37% (Hawaii). (See **Table B-5.**)

The upper threshold for the cost-effectiveness performance measure is 5.0 and the lower threshold is 2.0. In FY2011, South Dakota had a cost-effectiveness score of 10.41 and Louisiana had a score of 5.05. Even though there was a 5.36 percentage point difference between the two states, the applicable incentive percentage for those two states and the other 27 states with scores of at least 5.0 was 100%. In FY2011, only one jurisdiction (the Virgin Islands, 1.98) was below the lower threshold of 2.0. (See **Table B-5.**)

There have been several criticisms of the CSE performance thresholds,[46] namely that the upper thresholds are too low. Some observers contend that the numerical percentages of the thresholds were established in law almost 15 years ago and that they no longer represent a measure that challenges states. They argue that although you do not want an upper threshold that is unattainable, you do want one that will encourage states to improve their performance. Others note that because the thresholds were somewhat arbitrary to begin with, it is important to adjust them over time in order to challenge states to keep improving in the specified areas. It has also been mentioned that perhaps there should be an adjustment for population size as well as certain social and/or economic factors such as high level of nonmarital births in a state and low employment rates. In contrast, those who support the current performance standards say that it is unfair to raise the bar just because states are doing a good job. They contend that especially during these times of reduced resources, states are doing more with less and should not be penalized by increasing performance thresholds.

Should Incentive Payments be Based on Additional Performance Indicators?

The establishment and implementation of the current CSE incentive payment system was in part a recognition that a single indicator (i.e., cost-effectiveness) could not effectively evaluate the performance of the CSE program. The current CSE incentive payment system bases incentives on the state's success in achieving a number of goals, in addition to its ability to provide services in a cost-effective manner. Incentive payments are tied to the rates of paternity establishment, child support order establishment, collection of current child support payments, and collection of arrearages (past-due child support payments), as well as the amount of child support collected for each dollar spent (i.e., cost-effectiveness).

Some in the CSE community contend that several other indicators of performance have just as much legitimacy as the five measures that were enacted.[47] They include medical child support, interstate collections, welfare cost avoidance, payment processing performance, and customer service. In contrast, according to a report on the implementation of the CSE incentive payment system, many states indicated that the five measures were adequate and that adding new ones would be premature.[48]

Medical Child Support

P.L. 105-200 (enacted in 1998) established the revised CSE incentive payment system and also required the HHS Secretary, in consultation with state CSE directors and representatives of children potentially eligible for medical support, to develop a medical support incentive measure based on the state's effectiveness in establishing and enforcing medical child support obligations. The medical support incentive was to be part of the performance-based child support incentive system.[49] The 1998 law required that a report on this new incentive measure be submitted to Congress not later than October 1, 1999. Although a report was submitted (in March 1999), it recommended that the use of a medical support performance measure be postponed.[50]

To date, the CSE program has never had an incentive performance measure for medical child support. Although medical support data is collected by the states, that information is not currently used to compute incentive payments[51] or penalties and, according to OCSE, there are no immediate plans to use it in connection with the incentive payment system. A medical support incentive measure has been put on hold until OCSE provides further guidance.[52] Medical support data currently provided by states are not required to be determined complete and reliable based on an audit by OCSE.

It should also be noted that although incentive payments are additional income for state CSE programs, in that they are required to be reinvested into the CSE program (or a related activity), they are no longer matched with federal dollars.[53] Thus, their impact on the CSE program has been lessened.[54] In addition, beginning January 1, 2014, the Affordable Care Act (ACA, P.L. 111-148) is expected to expand health insurance coverage to millions of individuals through new health insurance exchanges and expansions in

Medicaid. Questions remain, however, regarding how the ACA will impact medical child support.[55]

Interstate Collections

Many CSE workers contend that the most difficult child support orders to establish and enforce are interstate cases. Although states are required to cooperate in interstate child support enforcement, problems arise due to the autonomy of local courts. Family law has traditionally been under the jurisdiction of state and local governments, and citizens fall under the jurisdiction of the courts where they live. Many child support advocates argue that a child should not be seriously disadvantaged in obtaining child support just because his or her parents do not live in the same state. Despite several federal enforcement tools intended to facilitate the establishment and enforcement of interstate collections, problems still exist. Given that about 33% of all CSE cases involve more than one state, some analysts maintain that a performance indicator that would measure whether states were successfully establishing and enforcing interstate child support cases would significantly improve the overall effectiveness of the CSE program.

Others acknowledge the importance of interstate collections but argue that states are not yet in a position to perform satisfactorily on an interstate performance measure. They acknowledge that although interstate collections increased by 52% over the thirteen-year period FY1998-FY2011, from $1.032 billion in FY1998 to $1.568 billion in FY2011, interstate collections (i.e., child support collections forwarded to other states) comprised 7% of total CSE collections in FY1998 and 6% of total CSE collections in FY2011.

Welfare Cost Avoidance

Unlike other social services programs, the CSE program is intended to transfer private—not public— funds to nonwelfare families enrolled in the program. Thus, the CSE program imposes personal responsibility on noncustodial parents by requiring them to meet their financial obligations to their children, thereby alleviating taxpayers of this responsibility. These child support payments often reduce government spending by providing families with incomes sufficient to make them ineligible for programs such as TANF.

In FY2009, child support payments enabled 217,000 CSE families to end their TANF eligibility. Research has indicated that families go on welfare less often and leave sooner when they receive reliable child support payments. In addition, federal costs for Medicaid, Supplemental Nutrition Assistance

Program (SNAP), and other means-tested programs decrease when both parents support their children.[56]

Although it is difficult to determine *how much* money might have been spent on various public assistance programs without the collection of child support payments, some analysts contend that it would be good public policy to add a performance indicator that attempts to measure—or at least estimate—the impact of CSE collections in reducing or eliminating costs in other public benefit/welfare programs.[57] Other analysts argue that adding a performance indicator to measure welfare cost avoidance would only add more complexity to an already complicated incentive payment system.

Payment Processing Performance

Some state policymakers and advocates want to look at an even broader set of factors when evaluating their state CSE program. They maintain that a legitimate purpose of performance standards in some instances is to set expectations. They contend that, because the CSE program has expanded its mission from welfare cost recovery to include promotion of self-sufficiency and personal responsibility and service delivery, it should account for payment processing performance. Such a measure would try to capture whether or not child support payments were accurately accounted, whether families were paid in a timely manner, and whether both custodial and noncustodial parents were satisfied with the state's CSE dispute resolution system.[58]

Should TANF Funds be Reduced Because of Poor CSE Performance?

Several persons who commented on the federal regulations for implementation of the CSE incentive payment and audit penalty provisions said that incentive payments and financial penalties are at odds with each other because they affect different programs (i.e., CSE and TANF).[59] Incentive payments are given to states from federal CSE funding and penalties are taken from a state's TANF funding.[60]

Historically, Congress has linked the CSE program and the TANF (and old AFDC) program. Currently Section 402(a)(2) of the Social Security Act (Title IV-A which deals with TANF (and used to pertain to the AFDC program)) stipulates that the Governor of a state must certify that it will operate an approved CSE program as a condition of receiving TANF block grant funding. Since the enactment of the CSE program in 1975, there has always been a provision in federal law that linked poor performance (and penalties) or noncompliance in the CSE program with a reduction in Title IV-A funding.

The principle that there are levels of state performance that would merit an incentive payment and there are levels that would warrant a penalty was incorporated into the current CSE incentive payment system. But, the law also provides that, before a penalty is imposed, states with lower performance levels may be able to receive some incentive, provided their program improves sufficiently and quickly.[61] States with poor performance are able to still qualify for an incentive payment if a significant increase over the previous year's performance is achieved in those measures (i.e., 10 percentage points on the paternity establishment performance level, 5 percentage points on the child support order establishment performance level, 5 percentage points on the current support collections performance level, and 5 percentage points on the arrearage collections performance level).

Federal law stipulates that with regard to the three "more important" performance measures, states must achieve certain levels of performance in order to avoid being penalized for poor performance. The three performance measures are: paternity establishment, child support order establishment, and collection of current child support payments. A graduated penalty equal to a 1% to 5% reduction in federal TANF block grant funds is assessed against states that fail to meet the CSE performance requirements.[62]

Although there is an interaction between the incentive payment and financial penalty systems, they affect different programs. Thus, even if a state's incentive payment is larger than any penalty assessed against the state, the state cannot easily reconcile the difference because the state is required to reinvest incentive payments back into the CSE program. The state would have to expend other state funds (that are not earmarked for the CSE program) to replace the loss in TANF funding.

An alternative to imposing penalties in the form of reducing TANF funding to a state for the inadequacies of its CSE program would be to reduce funding for the CSE program instead. This could be done by taking the financial penalty out of the state's incentive payment and/or subtracting the penalty from the federal government's 66% matching funds to the state.

Why Aren't the Incentives and Penalties Consistent for the Paternity Establishment Performance Measure?

Unlike the other performance measures, the paternity establishment indicator has two separate standards to which it must adhere. First, the Paternity Establishment Percentage (PEP), must meet a 90% standard (Section 452(g) of the Social Security Act). This means that federal law currently requires that states must establish paternity for at least 90% of the children who need to have their father legally identified in order to substantially comply with the requirements of the CSE program.[63]

If a state does not meet the PEP, it must raise its performance by a specified level of improvement in order to avoid having a financial penalty imposed. The percentage of improvement required varies with a state's performance level. The increase needed to avoid a penalty decreases with higher PEP scores until a state reaches a 90% or higher PEP, at which point the penalty is avoided without an increase in performance. For example, a state with a PEP of less than 40% needs a 6 percentage point increase over the prior year to avoid the penalty. Whereas, a state with a PEP between 75% and 90% needs a 2 percentage point increase over the previous year to avoid the penalty.[64] If the state fails to increase the PEP by the necessary percentage points after a corrective action period, the state is penalized by a 1%-5% reduction in its federal TANF funding.

Second, in a separate provision (Section 458 of the Social Security Act) the PEP is included as one of the five CSE performance measures. Thus, states can receive incentive payments if their PEP meets certain requirements. The incentive payment provision with respect to the PEP is consistent with the view of the CSE community that only poor performance should be penalized. Thus, under the incentive formula, an incentive is awarded to a state with a PEP of 50% or more. The incentive formula provides that a state that achieves a PEP of 80% or more will receive 100% of the applicable state collection's base for that measure. If a state has a PEP of less than 50%, the state must increase its PEP score by at least 10 percentage points over the previous year's score in order to receive an incentive payment.

From the outset of the performance measure debate (1996-1998), there was a concern about whether states should be subject to penalties and be eligible for incentives at the same time. Some argued that the lack of an incentive payment would make some states doubly penalized by not improving performance. It was decided that states should be eligible for incentive payments based on performance even if they were subject to penalties because their performance had not improved to the extent required to avoid the penalty.[65] The work group that developed the current incentive payment system maintained that the existing statutory PEP standard of 90% was too high and that it conflicted with their premise that only very poor performance should be penalized. Thus, the work group overlaid another provision on top of existing law which provided that a state that had a PEP of 80% or higher would receive 100% of the applicable state collection's base for the paternity establishment performance measure. This new PEP for incentive payment purposes created what many maintain is an inconsistency in CSE law.

According to the National Council of Child Support Directors:

> It is inconsistent to reward a state that achieves a paternity establishment percentage of 80% with maximum child support incentive funding, but impose a penalty against the State's TANF funding if a 2 percentage point increase is not achieved between 80% and 90% performance.[66]

The National Council of Child Support Directors recommended that "the paternity establishment penalty provisions set the upper threshold at 80%, which will then make it consistent and uniform with the existing incentive formula under which a state that has a paternity establishment percentage of 80% or more receives 100% of the weight allowable for that measure."[67] If this recommendation was enacted into law, states would be required to establish paternity for at least 80% of the children who need to have their father legally identified rather than 90% (as required by current law).

Should Incentive Payments be Based on Individual State Performance Rather than Aggregate State Performance?

The CSE incentive payment system adds an element of uncertainty to what used to be a somewhat predictable source of income for states. Although in the aggregate, states receive higher incentive payments than under the earlier incentive payment system, these totals are a fixed amount, and individual states have to compete with each other for their share of the capped funds. The capped incentive payment system creates an interactive effect—an increase in incentive payments to one state must be matched by a decrease in payments to other states. Similarly, if one state's performance weakens or the state fails an audit, every other state obtains an increase in incentive payments.

Although CSE incentive payments were constructed to compare a state's program performance to itself rather than a "national average," the fixed amount of aggregate incentive payments forces a state to compete with the other states for its share of the aggregate amount.[68]

Under the current incentive system, whether or not a state receives an incentive payment for good performance and the total amount of the incentive payment depend on four factors: the total amount of money available in a given fiscal year from which to make incentive payments, the state's success in obtaining collections on behalf of its caseload, the state's performance in five areas, and the relative success or failure of other states in making collections and meeting these performance criteria. Because the incentive payments are now capped, some states face a loss of incentive payments even if they improve their performance.

Some analysts argue that each state is unique in terms of its CSE caseload and thereby should only have to make improvements over its own performance in previous years with regard to rewarding of incentive payments.[69] Nevertheless, CSE programs are compared to one another in that there is a capped funding source and it must be shared by all. So even though Texas has a large CSE caseload, shares an international border, and has vast cultural and socioeconomic diversity among its residents, its program is in essence compared to that of a small mid-western state or a wealthy northeastern state in determining its share of CSE incentive dollars.

Others contend that if a state deems that it has not received a sufficient amount of incentive payments and that more CSE funding is necessary, it is the state's prerogative to augment federal funding. They maintain that the federal government is carrying too much of the financial burden of the CSE program. They point out that the federal government matches state funds at a 66% rate and additionally provides states with incentive payments.

Will the Elimination of the Federal Match of Incentive Payments Adversely Affect CSE Programs?

As mentioned earlier, the CSE funding structure requires states to spend state dollars on the program in order to receive federal matching funds. CSE incentive payments in past years[70] had been an important source of those state dollars.

Under previous law, the regular 66% federal match on the incentive payment resulted in a substantial increase in state CSE funding—in that for every dollar the state reinvested in the CSE program, the federal government matched that investment with about $2.[71] Thereby, before FY2008 and in FY2009 and FY2010, states were able to significantly leverage their investment through the federal financial structure. For example, in FY2010, actual incentive payments to states amounted to $504 million; the federal match (at the 66% rate) on the incentive payments amounted to almost twice that figure, $978 million, which translated into the state spending $1.482 billion (based solely on incentive payments) on CSE activities.[72] The elimination of federal reimbursement of CSE incentive payments may result in a significant reduction in CSE financing in the future.

It is generally agreed that state spending/investment in the CSE program significantly impacts program performance. Several past studies indicated that most of the best-performing state CSE programs also had the most generous funding levels.[73] Moreover, "Research has shown that reductions in program expenditures due to funding shortfalls negatively affect program performance particularly in regards to labor-intensive initiatives such as support order establishment, arrears collection initiatives, intensive work with hard-to-serve customers, and empoyer initiatives."[74] The elimination of the federal match of incentive payments is expected to reduce overall CSE program expenditures and correspondingly reduce the rate of growth of child support collections. The OCSE expects that while some states will increase their state contributions to cover some of the lost federal funds, they will not completely make up the shortfall and overall CSE expenditures will be reduced.[75]

According to a 2011 Government Accountability Office (GAO) report:

> Several state officials we interviewed confirmed that they were using the reinstated incentive match funds to sustain program operations and avoid layoffs during tight state budget climates. This is unlike prior years, when incentive match funds might have been used for long-term projects because funding was more predictable. Looking to the future, several of the state officials we interviewed described funding uncertainty surrounding the expiration of the incentive match in fiscal year 2011, as well as state budget situations. Not knowing whether the incentive match will be extended again or how much their future state CSE appropriations will be has made planning more difficult. Several officials emphasized that even states that maintained overall expenditure levels when the incentive match was eliminated in fiscal year 2008 may not be able to do so again in fiscal year 2011, as many state budget situations have worsened since the economic recession. Some officials also noted that the delivery of services beyond the core mission of the CSE program—such as job skills training and fatherhood initiatives—is

particularly uncertain. These officials also told us that, although they believe that these services and partnerships are necessary to continue increasing their collections, particularly from noncustodial parents who are underemployed or have barriers to maintaining employment, these services would be reduced to preserve core services in the event of dramatic budget shortfalls.[76]

Many in the CSE community argue that any reduction in the federal government's financial commitment to the CSE system could negatively affect states' ability to serve families.[77] They contend that a cost shift to the states (during a time when many interests are competing for limited state dollars) could jeopardize the effectiveness of the CSE program and thereby could have a negative impact on the children and families the CSE program is designed to serve.

APPENDIX A. LEGISLATIVE HISTORY OF CSE INCENTIVE PAYMENTS

Before enactment of the CSE program in 1975, when a state or locality collected child support payments from a noncustodial parent on behalf of a family receiving Aid to Families with Dependent Children (AFDC), the federal government was reimbursed for its share of the cost of AFDC payments to the family.[78] Although local units of government (e.g., counties) often enforced child support obligations, in most states they did not make any financial contributions toward funding AFDC benefit payments. Therefore the localities were not eligible for any share of the "savings" that occurred when child support was collected from a noncustodial parent on behalf of an AFDC family. From the debate on the establishment of a CSE program, Congress concluded that a fiscal sharing in the results of child support collections could be a strong incentive for encouraging the local units of government to improve their CSE activities.[79]

P.L. 90-248, Social Security Amendments of 1967 (January 2, 1968)

Although the formal CSE program was not in existence, P.L. 90-248 provided for the development and implementation of a program under which a state agency would undertake the responsibility for (1) determining the paternity of children receiving AFDC and who were born outside of marriage, and (2) securing financial support from the noncustodial parent for these and other children receiving AFDC, using reciprocal arrangements with other states to obtain and enforce court orders for support. (P.L. 89-97, the Social Security Amendments of 1965 (enacted July 30, 1965), allowed states to use the Federal Medical Assistance Percentage (FMAP) to determine federal-state cost sharing for Title IV-A (i.e., AFDC expenditures), which ranged from a minimum of 50% to a maximum of 83%.) Title IV-A included the child support enforcement provisions indicated above. This meant that if a state collected child support payments on behalf of an AFDC family, the federal government would be reimbursed at the state's FMAP. If the state had an FMAP of 60%, the federal government was reimbursed $60 for every $100 the state collected (from the noncustodial parent) in child support payments for AFDC families.

P.L. 93-647, Enactment of the CSE Program[80] (January 4, 1975)

P.L. 93-647 required that if a child support collection were made by any locality in the state or by the state for another state, that locality or state was to receive a special bonus—incentive payment—based on the amount of any child support collected from a noncustodial parent to reimburse amounts paid out as AFDC. The incentive payment was equal to 25% of the amount of child support collected on behalf of AFDC families for the first 12 months and 10% thereafter. The incentive payment came out of the federal share of the child support recovered (i.e., collected) on behalf AFDC families.[81]

P.L. 95-30, Tax Reduction and Simplification Act of 1977 (May 23, 1977)

P.L. 95-30 changed the rate at which incentives were paid to states and localities for child support collections used to reimburse AFDC payments. This amendment to Section 458 of the Social Security Act simplified the complex process of computing incentive payments at two different rates by adopting a flat 15% incentive payment rate. The incentive payment was now equal to 15% of child support collections made on behalf of AFDC families. The incentive payment came out of the federal share of the child support recovered (i.e., collected) on behalf AFDC families.

P.L. 97-248, Tax Equity and Fiscal Responsibility Act of 1982 (September 3, 1982)

P.L. 97-248 reduced the incentive payment rate from 15% of child support collections made on behalf of AFDC families to 12% of child support collections made on behalf of AFDC families. The incentive payment came out of the federal share of the child support recovered (i.e., collected) on behalf AFDC families.

P.L. 98-378, Child Support Enforcement Amendments of 1984 (August 16, 1984)

P.L. 98-378 significantly revised incentive payments. Instead of making incentive payments to localities and states that collected child support payments on another state's behalf, the federal government made the incentive payments directly to the states[82] and each state was required to pass incentive payments through to local CSE agencies if those agencies shared in funding the state CSE program. In order to improve cost-effectiveness and encourage states to emphasize child support collections on behalf of both AFDC and non-AFDC families, the incentive payment formula was changed so that states were paid a minimum of 6% of their child support collections in AFDC cases and 6% of their child support collections in non-AFDC cases. Under this approach, there was the potential to earn up to 10% of both AFDC and non-AFDC child support collections depending on the state's cost-effectiveness in running a child support program (i.e., ratio of state collections to the state's cost of operating the CSE program). The federal government paid the incentive payments from its share of retained collections for AFDC families and capped the amount of incentive payments any state could earn on the non-AFDC cases at 115%[83] of the AFDC incentive payment earned. The incentive payments came out of the federal share of the child support recovered (i.e., collected) on behalf AFDC families.

P.L. 100-485, Family Support Act of 1988 (October 13, 1988)

P.L. 100-485 included a provision that authorized Congress to create a U.S. Commission on Interstate Child Support to make recommendations to Congress on improving the child support program. That Commission's report called for a study of the federal funding formula and changes to an incentive structure that is based on performance. In addition, other national organizations, including the National Conference of State Legislatures, the American Public Welfare Association (now the American Public Human Services Association, APHSA), the National Governors Association, and several national advocacy organizations recommended the adoption of a new performance-based incentive system.[84]

P.L. 104-193, The 1996 Welfare Reform Law (August 22, 1996)

The Personal Responsibility and Work Opportunity Reconciliation Act of 1996 (P.L. 104-193) required the HHS Secretary, in consultation with state CSE program directors, to recommend to Congress a new incentive funding system for state CSE programs based on program performance. P.L. 104-193 required that (1) the new incentive funding system be developed in a revenue-neutral manner; (2) the new system provide additional payments to any state based on that state's performance; and (3) the Secretary report to Congress on the proposed new system by March 1, 1997.

The Incentive Funding Workgroup was formed in October 1996. This group consisted of 15 state and local CSE directors or their representatives and 11 federal staff representatives from HHS. Earlier efforts of this state-federal partnership produced the National Strategic Plan for the CSE program and a set of outcome measures to indicate the program's success in achieving the goals and objectives of the plan. Using the same collaboration and consensus-building approach, state and federal partners recommended a new incentive funding system based on the foundation of the CSE National Strategic Plan.

Over a period of three months, recommendations for the new incentive funding system emerged. State partners consulted with state CSE programs not represented directly on the Workgroup. The final recommendations represented a consensus among state and federal partners on the new incentive funding system. The Secretary fully endorsed the incentive formula recommendations. The Secretary's report made recommendations for a new CSE incentive payment system to the House Committee on Ways and Means and the Senate Committee on Finance.[85]

P.L. 105-200, Child Support Performance and Incentive Act of 1998 (July 16, 1998)

Most of the HHS Secretary's recommendations for a new incentive payment system were included in P.L. 105-200. This law replaced the old incentive payment system to states with a revised revenue-neutral incentive payment system that provides (1) incentive payments based on a percentage of the state's collections; (2) incorporation of five performance measures related to establishment of paternity and child support orders, collections of current and past-due support payments, and cost-effectiveness; (3) phase-in of the incentive system, with it being fully effective beginning in FY2002; (4) mandatory reinvestment of incentive payments into the CSE program (or an activity that contributes to improving the effectiveness or efficiency of the CSE program); and (5) an incentive payment formula weighted in favor of TANF and former TANF families.

P.L. 105-200 required the HHS Secretary to make incentive payments to the states and stipulated that the aggregate incentive payment to the states could not exceed the following amounts: $422 million for FY2000, $429 million for FY2001, $450 million for FY2002,[86] $461 million for FY2003, $454 million for FY2004, $446 million for FY2005, $458 million for FY2006, $471 million for FY2007, and $483 million for FY2008. For years after FY2008, the aggregate incentive payment to the states is to be increased to account for inflation.

P.L. 109-171, Deficit Reduction Act of 2005 (February 8, 2006)

P.L. 109-171 included a provision that eliminated (effective October 1, 2007, i.e., FY2008) the 66% federal match on CSE incentive payments that states, in compliance with federal law, reinvested back into the CSE program.

P.L. 111-5, the American Recovery and Reinvestment Act of 2009 (February 17, 2009)

P.L. 111-5 temporarily reinstated federal matching of incentive payments for FY2009 and FY2010.

APPENDIX B. TABLES

Appendix B includes several detailed state tables. Table B-1 shows that all states received incentive payments in FY2002, FY2005, FY2010, and FY2011 and the amounts they received. Table B-2 displays unaudited incentive performance scores for each of the five performance measures for FY2002. Table B-3 displays unaudited incentive performance scores for each of the five performance measures for FY2005. Table B-4 displays unaudited incentive performance scores for each of the five performance measures for FY2010. Table B-5 displays unaudited incentive performance scores for each of the five performance measures for FY2011.[87]

Table B-1. Actual Incentive Payments, by State, FY2002, FY2005, FY2010, and FY2011

(arranged by state with the highest incentive payment to state with the lowest incentive payment)

	State	FY2002	State	FY2005	State	FY2010	State	FY2011
1	California	36,814,328	California	41,743,556	Texas	55,115,303	Texas	59,639,748
2	Texas	33,815,354	Texas	37,594,823	California	37,940,293	California	37,894,749
3	Ohio	32,204,888	Ohio	28,985,608	Florida	29,999,032	Florida	33,054,957
4	Pennsylvania	30,284,824	New York	26,242,919	Ohio	29,151,769	New York	28,574,341
5	New York	30,176,739	Michigan	26,035,157	New York	27,395,346	Pennsylvania	26,492,989
6	Michigan	30,128,156	Pennsylvania	25,422,058	Pennsylvania	25,591,364	Michigan	24,466,511
7	Florida	21,261,888	Florida	25,263,730	Michigan	25,178,161	Ohio	22,197,109
8	New Jersey	17,367,328	New Jersey	15,974,982	New Jersey	17,170,697	New Jersey	17,015,753
9	Wisconsin	15,924,085	Wisconsin	13,748,475	Illinois	13,860,612	Illinois	15,775,485
10	Washington	15,204,033	North Carolina	13,461,627	Wisconsin	13,642,213	North Carolina	14,789,831
11	Minnesota	13,555,076	Washington	12,719,377	Georgia	13,476,091	Georgia	13,870,407
12	Georgia	11,999,643	Minnesota	12,135,231	Washington	12,605,105	Wisconsin	13,535,312
13	North Carolina	11,741,877	Georgia	10,808,188	Missouri	12,250,352	Washington	12,617,216

Table B-1. (Continued)

	State	FY2002	State	FY2005	State	FY2010	State	FY2011
14	Virginia	11,212,586	Virginia	10,237,234	Indiana	12,201,979	Missouri	12,098,575
15	Massachusetts	9,717,960	Missouri	10,204,439	Minnesota	12,093,695	Minnesota	11,907,544
16	Maryland	8,749,496	Massachusetts	8,898,038	Virginia	11,496,244	Virginia	11,633,569
17	Missouri	8,496,830	Illinois	8,650,633	North Carolina	11,190,271	Indiana	11,560,438
18	Kentucky	8,088,515	Indiana	8,385,495	Massachusetts	10,190,207	Massachusetts	10,647,319
19	Iowa	7,126,528	Tennessee	7,837,795	Tennessee	10,122,576	Tennessee	10,314,981
20	Tennessee	6,811,758	Maryland	7,303,489	Kentucky	7,967,078	Louisiana	8,029,653
21	Oregon	6,541,362	Iowa	6,917,274	Louisiana	7,578,061	Kentucky	7,836,843
22	Illinois	6,183,369	Louisiana	6,213,377	Iowa	7,482,967	Iowa	7,375,772
23	Indiana	5,564,581	Oregon	5,600,727	Maryland	7,169,234	Maryland	7,268,619
24	Connecticut	5,491,503	Arizona	5,423,112	Arizona	6,693,262	Oklahoma	6,433,082
25	Colorado	5,356,965	Kentucky	5,208,111	Oregon	6,173,524	Arizona	6,422,506
26	Arizona	5,206,147	Connecticut	4,865,914	Oklahoma	5,896,756	Oregon	6,238,714
27	Louisiana	4,389,087	Colorado	4,750,251	Colorado	5,300,432	Colorado	5,246,427
28	West Virginia	4,058,389	Alabama	4,020,646	Connecticut	5,166,296	Connecticut	5,058,826
29	South Carolina	3,899,715	West Virginia	3,879,643	West Virginia	4,702,120	Arkansas	4,723,619
30	Arkansas	3,217,437	Oklahoma	3,643,878	Arkansas	4,588,159	Alabama	4,612,658
31	Puerto Rico	3,201,676	Nebraska	3,475,303	South Carolina	4,543,448	Nebraska	4,605,084
32	Utah	3,101,832	South Carolina	3,321,883	Alabama	4,486,109	South Carolina	4,550,967
33	Nebraska	3,056,992	Kansas	3,289,970	Nebraska	4,380,112	Puerto Rico	4,341,887
34	Alabama	2,900,775	Utah	3,288,628	Puerto Rico	4,360,872	Mississippi	4,130,182
35	Oklahoma	2,899,609	Puerto Rico	3,268,672	Kansas	3,946,123	West Virginia	4,098,556
36	Kansas	2,873,656	Mississippi	3,222,870	Mississippi	3,879,458	Kansas	3,990,204
37	Maine	2,596,197	Arkansas	2,490,610	Utah	3,580,240	Utah	3,863,279
38	Mississippi	2,526,611	Idaho	2,389,857	Idaho	2,827,522	Nevada	3,122,406

	State	FY2002	State	FY2005	State	FY2010	State	FY2011
39	Alaska	1,679,107	Maine	2,167,195	Nevada	2,806,180	Idaho	2,791,858
40	South Dakota	1,656,493	Nevada	1,826,744	Maine	2,063,954	North Dakota	2,027,445
41	Idaho	1,650,232	Alaska	1,809,329	North Dakota	1,973,912	Maine	2,013,957
42	New Hampshire	1,438,353	New Hampshire	1,650,128	South Dakota	1,815,004	New Mexico	1,996,326
43	Montana	1,202,605	North Dakota	1,560,854	New Mexico	1,808,304	South Dakota	1,917,362
44	Wyoming	1,201,957	South Dakota	1,466,513	Alaska	1,778,401	Alaska	1,827,200
45	North Dakota	1,192,916	Hawaii	1,431,973	New Hampshire	1,733,474	New Hampshire	1,736,226
46	Vermont	1,127,161	Rhode Island	1,211,250	Hawaii	1,625,717	Hawaii	1,664,091
47	Delaware	1,034,185	Wyoming	1,163,702	Wyoming	1,286,050	Wyoming	1,311,261
48	Rhode Island	1,016,821	New Mexico	1,055,389	Delaware	1,262,780	Rhode Island	1,260,809
49	Hawaii	973,201	Montana	1,028,469	Rhode Island	1,204,315	Montana	1,194,604
50	Nevada	857,000	Vermont	977,267	Montana	1,131,812	Delaware	1,169,480
51	New Mexico	554,604	Delaware	900,305	Vermont	915,231	District of Columbia	912,555
52	District of Columbia	502,393	District of Columbia	598,507	District of Columbia	902,209	Vermont	891,151
53	Guam	101,209	Guam	119,823	Guam	192,683	Guam	171,983
54	Virgin Islands	63,968	Virgin Islands	108,972	Virgin Islands	106,891	Virgin Islands	77,575
	Total	$450,000,000	Total	$446,000,000	Total	$504,000,000	Total	$513,000,000

Source: Table prepared by the Congressional Research Service based on data from the Office of Child Support Enforcement, Department of Health and Human Services.

Note: The table shows the rank order of each state from state with the highest incentive payment (ranked 1) to the state with the lowest incentive payment (ranked 54). The four jurisdictions of the District of Columbia, Guam, Puerto Rico, and the Virgin Islands are included in the state totals.

Table B-2. Unaudited Child Support Enforcement Incentive Performance Scores, FY2002
(arranged by highest performing state to lowest performing state)

State	Paternity Establishment Percentage	State	Cases with Orders Percentage	State	Current Collections Percentage	State	Arrearage Cases Percentage	State	Cost-Effectiveness Score
Guam	452.87[a]	South Dakota	92.03	Pennsylvania	74.70	New Hampshire	71.58	Indiana	$7.80
Idaho	130.75	Washington	91.00	Minnesota	72.96	Pennsylvania	70.68	South Dakota	7.59
Montana	113.07	Iowa	87.79	Wisconsin	72.68	Vermont	70.64	Mississippi	7.12
Texas	108.43	Maine	87.17	North Dakota	71.55	South Dakota	68.59	Pennsylvania	6.85
California	107.94	Vermont	85.80	South Dakota	67.70	Washington	68.33	Hawaii	6.53
New Hampshire	106.74	Utah	85.11	Ohio	66.77	Delaware	67.83	Virginia	6.34
South Dakota	106.46	North Dakota	84.76	Nebraska	66.49	Ohio	67.46	Puerto Rico	6.27
Pennsylvania	106.01	Colorado	83.46	Vermont	66.34	Alaska	67.39	Wisconsin	6.11
Ohio	103.38	Montana	83.10	New Hampshire	65.51	North Dakota	66.12	South Carolina	5.87
Colorado	102.85	Pennsylvania	82.97	New York	65.12	Colorado	66.10	Oregon	5.85
Washington	100.88	Alaska	82.90	New Jersey	65.00	Utah	66.04	Massachusetts	5.77
Wyoming	97.78	Wyoming	82.75	Washington	63.98	Minnesota	65.07	Iowa	5.63
Illinois	97.06	New Hampshire	82.02	West Virginia	62.33	Texas	64.45	Texas	5.41
Maryland	96.67	Virginia	80.20	Maryland	62.02	Maryland	64.29	Idaho	5.29
Wisconsin	94.50	Wisconsin	78.99	North Carolina	61.26	Montana	63.72	Wyoming	5.00
Oregon	94.40	Missouri	78.93	Rhode Island	61.11	Iowa	63.34	Washington	4.95
Vermont	94.08	New Jersey	78.90	Delaware	60.74	Florida	62.83	Louisiana	4.87
Maine	93.56	Idaho	78.64	Oregon	60.41	Nevada	62.03	West Virginia	4.87
Michigan	92.04	Arkansas	78.53	Wyoming	60.05	Nebraska	61.66	New Jersey	4.83

State	Paternity Establishment Percentage	State	Cases with Orders Percentage	State	Current Collections Percentage	State	Arrearage Cases Percentage	State	Cost-Effectiveness Score
West Virginia	90.49	Minnesota	78.04	Texas	59.93	Wyoming	61.57	Ohio	4.81
Utah	90.27	Michigan	76.22	Massachusetts	59.68	Maine	61.25	Kentucky	4.71
Virginia	90.14	Nebraska	76.04	Michigan	59.36	New Jersey	61.18	North Dakota	4.71
Alaska	89.64	California	75.32	Iowa	59.10	Wisconsin	61.07	Missouri	4.63
Puerto Rico	88.17	West Virginia	74.90	Virginia	58.97	Oregon	61.04	Michigan	4.59
New York	87.77	North Carolina	73.15	Utah	58.60	Kansas	61.03	Rhode Island	4.52
Iowa	87.57	New York	73.05	Montana	58.50	Georgia	60.78	Tennessee	4.50
North Dakota	87.40	Ohio	71.38	Maine	57.76	Michigan	60.78	Alaska	4.49
Arkansas	85.88	Massachusetts	71.17	Louisiana	56.44	Louisiana	60.63	New York	4.49
Connecticut	85.06	Indiana	70.59	Florida	56.40	New York	60.43	North Carolina	4.43
North Carolina	84.41	Delaware	70.34	Idaho	55.43	New Mexico	60.33	New Hampshire	4.37
Georgia	83.25	Kentucky	70.04	Kansas	55.06	North Carolina	60.32	Maine	4.28
Kentucky	82.54	Oklahoma	69.69	Connecticut	55.04	Idaho	60.11	Arizona	4.25
Massachusetts	82.45	Texas	69.00	Colorado	54.97	Mississippi	59.84	Georgia	4.24
Minnesota	82.06	Maryland	68.65	Alaska	53.84	Massachusetts	58.32	Maryland	4.19
South Carolina	81.44	Georgia	68.16	Kentucky	52.80	Rhode Island	58.19	Montana	4.10
Hawaii	81.41	Louisiana	67.36	Hawaii	51.13	West Virginia	57.53	Minnesota	4.05
New Jersey	81.37	Arizona	66.99	Missouri	50.74	Oklahoma	56.78	Florida	4.03
Nebraska	81.03	Oregon	66.91	Tennessee	50.44	Virginia	56.37	Vermont	3.93
Oklahoma	80.69	South Carolina	66.71	Arkansas	50.32	Arkansas	55.53	Utah	3.89
Florida	80.10	Alabama	66.22	Georgia	49.73	California	54.92	Connecticut	3.76
Missouri	79.74	Florida	65.23	Mississippi	49.55	Tennessee	54.54	Colorado	3.66

Table B-2. (Continued)

State	Paternity Establishment Percentage	State	Cases with Orders Percentage	State	Current Collections Percentage	State	Arrearage Cases Percentage	State	Cost-Effectiveness Score
Delaware	77.21	Connecticut	64.34	South Carolina	49.51	Connecticut	53.13	Delaware	3.66
Tennessee	76.94	Kansas	63.91	Puerto Rico	48.67	Indiana	52.58	Alabama	3.64
Louisiana	76.83	Puerto Rico	63.76	Indiana	48.52	Illinois	52.30	Nebraska	2.87
Dist. of Columbia	75.23	Nevada	60.35	Dist. of Columbia	47.96	South Carolina	51.84	Nevada	2.87
Kansas	74.75	Hawaii	59.22	Alabama	47.77	Puerto Rico	50.84	Illinois	2.80
Mississippi	69.82	Tennessee	56.55	Virgin Islands	47.02	Arizona	50.63	Oklahoma	2.80
Rhode Island	68.85	Rhode Island	51.24	Nevada	46.99	Missouri	50.00	Dist. of Columbia	2.69
Nevada	67.89	Guam	50.17	New Mexico	46.75	Kentucky	49.97	Arkansas	2.66
Alabama	65.39	Mississippi	49.84	Oklahoma	46.46	Virgin Islands	48.69	Kansas	2.61
New Mexico	57.61	New Mexico	47.51	Arizona	44.48	Alabama	47.95	California	1.91
Virgin Islands	52.94	Illinois	40.82	Guam	43.16	Guam	37.08	Guam	1.64
Arizona	51.02	Virgin Islands	38.07	California	42.40	Hawaii	36.87	Virgin Islands	1.58
Indiana	50.83	Dist. of Columbia	29.66	Illinois	39.11	Dist. of Columbia	30.21	New Mexico	$1.46

Source: Table prepared by the Congressional Research Service based on data from the Office of Child Support Enforcement, Department of Health and Human Services.

Note: The paternity establishment percentage can be greater than 100% because states can take credit for paternities established for children of any age and compare that number established to the number of births outside of marriage for a single year.

a. Because of conflicting information and data in other reports Guam's PEP score of 452.87 was excluded from this report's analysis.

Table B-3. Unaudited Child Support Enforcement Incentive Performance Scores, FY2005
(arranged by highest performing state to lowest performing state)

State	Paternity Establishment Percentage	State	Cases with Orders Percentage	State	Current Collections Percentage	State	Arrearage Cases Percentage	State	Cost Effectiveness Score
Oklahoma	112.42	South Dakota	96.00	Pennsylvania	74.72	Pennsylvania	73.50	Indiana	$8.53
Maine	111.02	Alaska	92.41	North Dakota	72.70	New Hampshire	71.97	Mississippi	8.53
Texas	107.95	Washington	89.57	Minnesota	69.31	Vermont	71.01	South Dakota	7.76
California	106.54	Wyoming	89.38	South Dakota	69.04	North Dakota	69.69	South Carolina	7.07
Montana	105.43	Maine	89.10	Wisconsin	69.01	South Dakota	69.52	Texas	6.81
Alaska	104.79	Montana	88.12	Ohio	68.98	Wyoming	67.76	Michigan	6.70
Puerto Rico	104.40	Vermont	88.02	Nebraska	67.84	Utah	67.57	Virginia	6.52
Ohio	104.13	North Dakota	86.75	Vermont	66.98	Alaska	67.46	Rhode Island	6.45
South Dakota	103.56	Colorado	85.38	New Jersey	65.27	Florida	66.71	Pennsylvania	6.39
North Dakota	102.88	Iowa	85.35	New York	65.13	Ohio	66.54	Wyoming	6.25
New Hampshire	102.53	Utah	85.25	Iowa	64.74	Washington	66.11	North Dakota	6.03
New Jersey	100.45	Pennsylvania	84.71	New Hampshire	64.63	Minnesota	66.08	Puerto Rico	6.01
Wisconsin	100.23	Virginia	84.68	North Carolina	64.52	Iowa	65.70	Kentucky	5.95
Florida	99.90	Wisconsin	83.55	Massachusetts	63.79	Colorado	65.65	Massachusetts	5.93
Vermont	98.82	West Virginia	83.54	West Virginia	63.69	Texas	65.23	Oregon	5.93
Pennsylvania	98.73	Arkansas	82.41	Wyoming	63.67	Nebraska	64.96	Iowa	5.80
Hawaii	98.09	Texas	82.23	Washington	63.31	Wisconsin	64.19	Ohio	5.66
North Carolina	96.37	Minnesota	82.12	Maryland	63.08	Montana	64.14	Idaho	5.58

Table B-3. (Continued)

State	Paternity Establishment Percentage	State	Cases with Orders Percentage	State	Current Collections Percentage	State	Arrearage Cases Percentage	State	Cost Effectiveness Score
Minnesota	96.09	Missouri	81.63	Utah	61.39	Maryland	63.92	Tennessee	5.44
Washington	95.16	New Hampshire	81.15	Virginia	60.91	Delaware	63.71	Missouri	5.41
Iowa	94.76	North Carolina	80.88	Montana	60.68	New Jersey	63.20	Wisconsin	5.41
Idaho	93.97	New Jersey	80.72	Rhode Island	60.63	West Virginia	62.88	Georgia	5.20
Kentucky	92.53	California	80.28	Michigan	60.52	Kansas	62.59	North Carolina	5.10
Missouri	92.52	New York	80.03	Texas	60.51	North Carolina	62.16	West Virginia	4.90
Colorado	92.36	Idaho	78.58	Delaware	60.41	New Mexico	61.32	Maryland	4.88
Illinois	92.19	Nebraska	77.72	Maine	60.30	Arkansas	60.87	Florida	4.80
Oregon	91.71	Kentucky	77.51	Oregon	60.09	Oregon	60.72	New York	4.79
Massachusetts	91.22	Maryland	74.65	Colorado	57.69	Mississippi	60.46	New Hampshire	4.75
Kansas	91.19	Michigan	74.50	Arkansas	57.09	Tennessee	60.05	New Jersey	4.74
Arkansas	90.57	Georgia	74.47	Florida	56.72	Georgia	59.16	Washington	4.74
Maryland	90.57	Kansas	74.41	Idaho	55.81	New York	59.02	Arizona	4.73
New York	90.33	Alabama	73.93	Virgin Islands	55.66	Rhode Island	58.03	Louisiana	4.71
Virginia	89.34	Arizona	73.91	Louisiana	55.45	Indiana	58.01	Alaska	4.54
Connecticut	87.87	Delaware	73.83	Tennessee	55.43	Massachusetts	57.86	Hawaii	4.39
West Virginia	87.65	Massachusetts	73.60	Connecticut	55.38	Virginia	57.76	Maine	4.27
Michigan	86.46	Ohio	72.69	Kentucky	55.31	Louisiana	57.64	Alabama	4.26
South Carolina	84.67	Florida	72.18	Hawaii	55.30	California	56.03	Minnesota	4.22

State	Paternity Establishment Percentage	State	Cases with Orders Percentage	State	Current Collections Percentage	State	Arrearage Cases Percentage	State	Cost Effectiveness Score
Georgia	83.69	Louisiana	71.99	Puerto Rico	55.28	Connecticut	55.51	Utah	4.03
Utah	83.47	South Carolina	71.23	Alaska	54.96	Oklahoma	55.18	Montana	4.02
Wyoming	82.90	Connecticut	69.52	Missouri	54.69	Idaho	54.66	Vermont	3.91
Nebraska	82.49	Indiana	69.39	Kansas	54.52	South Carolina	53.80	Oklahoma	3.79
Indiana	82.28	Oklahoma	69.09	Mississippi	53.47	Kentucky	53.44	Arkansas	3.68
Louisiana	81.93	Oregon	67.41	Illinois	53.29	Michigan	53.18	Colorado	3.68
Alabama	81.89	Puerto Rico	66.37	Dist. of Columbia	52.89	Maine	52.96	Connecticut	3.68
Arizona	81.11	Tennessee	64.84	Indiana	52.82	Puerto Rico	52.55	Illinois	3.68
Tennessee	80.48	Nevada	62.41	Georgia	52.56	Missouri	52.10	Nebraska	3.57
Virgin Islands	79.56	Guam	60.18	Alabama	51.74	Arizona	51.37	Kansas	3.39
Guam	79.27	New Mexico	59.83	Oklahoma	50.11	Guam	50.33	Delaware	3.10
Delaware	79.14	Illinois	59.35	New Mexico	50.00	Alabama	49.96	Nevada	2.98
Mississippi	77.80	Hawaii	58.30	California	49.27	Nevada	49.60	Dist. of Columbia	2.45
Rhode Island	77.02	Rhode Island	57.18	South Carolina	47.41	Virgin Islands	47.78	California	2.15
Dist. of Columbia	74.81	Virgin Islands	55.41	Guam	47.33	Illinois	45.91	Guam	2.11
Nevada	66.30	Mississippi	53.63	Nevada	45.68	Dist. of Columbia	43.68	Virgin Islands	2.11
New Mexico	54.05	Dist. of Columbia	39.60	Arizona	44.36	Hawaii	41.36	New Mexico	$2.10

Source: Table prepared by the Congressional Research Service based on data from the Office of Child Support Enforcement, Department of Health and Human Services.

Note: The paternity establishment percentage can be greater than 100% because states can take credit for paternities established for children of any age and compare that number established to the number of births outside of marriage for a single year.

Table B–4. Unaudited Child Support Enforcement Incentive Performance Scores, FY2010
(arranged by highest performing state to lowest performing state)

State	Paternity Establishment Percentage	State	Cases with Orders Percentage	State	Current Collections Percentage	State	Arrearage Cases Percentage	State	Cost Effectiveness Score
Arizona	118.29	South Dakota	92.38	Pennsylvania	83.24	Pennsylvania	83.14	Wyoming	$12.54
Montana	108.31	Wyoming	91.00	North Dakota	74.21	West Virginia	71.40	South Dakota	11.34
North Dakota	108.14	Vermont	90.05	Wisconsin	70.58	Minnesota	70.02	Puerto Rico	10.23
New Hampshire	107.10	Pennsylvania	89.90	Iowa	69.75	Colorado	69.65	Texas	8.80
Oklahoma	106.99	North Dakota	89.78	Minnesota	69.63	Vermont	69.18	Indiana	7.43
Maine	105.11	Washington	89.47	Nebraska	68.99	Wyoming	68.91	Kentucky	6.84
West Virginia	104.91	Alaska	89.44	South Dakota	68.88	Iowa	68.82	Virginia	6.83
South Dakota	104.37	Kentucky	88.69	Massachusetts	67.89	New Hampshire	68.82	Missouri	6.71
Vermont	104.03	Maine	88.35	Vermont	67.62	North Dakota	68.70	Tennessee	6.68
California	102.57	Colorado	88.09	New York	66.95	Georgia	68.17	Georgia	6.58
Indiana	102.16	Montana	87.61	Ohio	66.62	Nebraska	68.05	Michigan	6.55
Washington	101.44	Utah	87.56	Washington	65.79	New Mexico	67.11	Ohio	6.54
Minnesota	100.39	Missouri	86.45	North Carolina	65.21	South Dakota	66.76	Idaho	6.03
Nevada	100.30	Virginia	86.39	Wyoming	65.14	Arkansas	66.43	Iowa	6.02
Wisconsin	100.17	West Virginia	86.21	New Jersey	65.05	Alaska	65.89	Arizona	5.84
North Carolina	99.80	Wisconsin	85.33	Maryland	64.46	Montana	65.86	Wisconsin	5.81
Pennsylvania	98.21	Minnesota	85.27	West Virginia	64.20	Utah	64.89	Mississippi	5.74
Puerto Rico	97.67	Iowa	85.06	Texas	63.44	Texas	64.51	Pennsylvania	5.68

State	Paternity Establishment Percentage	State	Cases with Orders Percentage	State	Current Collections Percentage	State	Arrearage Cases Percentage	State	Cost Effectiveness Score
Colorado	97.37	New Hampshire	85.05	Colorado	62.70	Indiana	64.14	North Dakota	5.61
Utah	97.22	Arkansas	84.73	Michigan	62.45	Ohio	64.01	North Carolina	5.36
Arkansas	97.22	Georgia	84.33	Arkansas	62.31	North Carolina	63.67	Oregon	5.29
New Jersey	95.64	Nebraska	83.88	Virginia	61.96	Guam	63.57	Florida	5.12
Virginia	95.51	Arizona	83.79	Hawaii	61.58	Kansas	63.30	West Virginia	5.03
Hawaii	95.19	Maryland	82.82	Guam	60.99	Washington	62.87	Massachusetts	4.87
Nebraska	94.82	California	82.55	Utah	60.97	New Jersey	62.40	Nebraska	4.84
Alabama	94.76	Idaho	82.43	New Hampshire	60.94	Wisconsin	62.09	South Carolina	4.80
Texas	94.69	Alabama	82.36	Montana	60.80	Maryland	61.57	Louisiana	4.69
Kentucky	94.48	Texas	82.06	Georgia	60.67	Oklahoma	61.35	New York	4.69
Michigan	94.25	Massachusetts	81.90	Maine	60.41	Illinois	61.33	Illinois	4.56
Connecticut	93.91	North Carolina	81.18	Rhode Island	60.35	Massachusetts	60.70	Washington	4.43
Ohio	93.90	New Jersey	80.95	Alaska	59.98	Virginia	60.48	New Jersey	4.37
New Mexico	93.13	Kansas	80.31	Delaware	59.96	California	60.29	Hawaii	4.36
Rhode Island	92.90	New York	80.05	Oregon	59.29	Florida	59.93	Montana	4.31
Massachusetts	92.89	Michigan	79.16	Connecticut	58.48	Mississippi	59.65	Alabama	4.28
Alaska	92.68	Louisiana	78.47	Indiana	58.28	Oregon	59.30	Utah	4.21
Iowa	92.57	Ohio	77.70	Dist. of Columbia	58.09	Connecticut	59.26	Colorado	4.19
Georgia	92.52	Illinois	77.66	Idaho	58.06	New York	59.15	New Hampshire	4.18
Oregon	92.19	Puerto Rico	77.10	Kentucky	57.92	Kentucky	58.96	Alaska	4.11
Florida	91.46	Guam	77.05	Illinois	57.85	Missouri	58.25	Oklahoma	4.03
Illinois	90.77	Nevada	76.48	Missouri	56.70	Maine	58.03	Maine	3.80

Table B-4. (Continued)

State	Paternity Establishment Percentage	State	Cases with Orders Percentage	State	Current Collections Percentage	State	Arrearage Cases Percentage	State	Cost Effectiveness Score
Missouri	90.65	Indiana	75.99	Louisiana	56.65	Delaware	58.01	Connecticut	3.71
Idaho	90.64	Oregon	74.71	Puerto Rico	56.63	Tennessee	57.45	Minnesota	3.70
New York	90.60	Oklahoma	74.62	Virgin Islands	55.98	Louisiana	57.31	Arkansas	3.68
Kansas	90.51	Florida	73.50	California	55.96	Idaho	57.25	Maryland	3.58
South Carolina	90.46	Connecticut	73.22	Mississippi	55.30	Michigan	57.10	Kansas	3.41
Tennessee	90.28	Hawaii	69.29	Kansas	55.26	Nevada	56.80	Vermont	3.37
Louisiana	90.27	Tennessee	68.88	New Mexico	54.97	Rhode Island	56.05	Rhode Island	3.31
Virgin Islands	90.26	New Mexico	68.34	Oklahoma	54.74	Alabama	55.42	Delaware	3.22
Maryland	89.47	Delaware	67.09	Florida	52.16	Arizona	54.14	Nevada	2.92
Guam	88.60	South Carolina	66.75	South Carolina	51.89	South Carolina	54.01	Guam	2.66
Dist. of Columbia	88.35	Rhode Island	64.96	Tennessee	51.87	Puerto Rico	53.29	New Mexico	2.54
Wyoming	84.99	Dist. of Columbia	64.76	Arizona	50.82	Virgin Islands	51.39	California	2.38
Mississippi	82.09	Virgin Islands	63.03	Alabama	50.20	Dist. of Columbia	49.71	Dist. of Columbia	2.10
Delaware	81.26	Mississippi	56.87	Nevada	49.10	Hawaii	45.61	Virgin Islands	$1.42

Source: Table prepared by the Congressional Research Service based on data from the Office of Child Support Enforcement, Department of Health and Human Services.

Note: The paternity establishment percentage can be greater than 100% because states can take credit for paternities established for children of any age and compare that number established to the number of births outside of marriage for a single year.

Table B-5. Unaudited Child Support Enforcement Incentive Performance Scores, FY2011
(arranged by highest performing state to lowest performing state)

State	Paternity Establishment Percentage	State	Cases with Orders Percentage	State	Current Collections Percentage	State	Arrearage Cases Percentage	State	Cost Effectiveness Score
Arizona	126.33	South Dakota	93.06	Pennsylvania	83.90	Pennsylvania	83.77	South Dakota	$10.41
Oklahoma	112.76	Wyoming	92.50	North Dakota	74.57	Wyoming	72.18	Mississippi	9.79
North Dakota	109.50	Alaska	91.76	Iowa	71.66	Minnesota	70.53	Massachusetts	9.45
Nevada	109.30	North Dakota	89.84	Wisconsin	70.59	Iowa	70.27	Texas	9.29
South Dakota	108.22	Washington	89.77	Minnesota	70.48	Vermont	69.96	Puerto Rico	8.86
Montana	107.05	Maine	89.74	Nebraska	69.75	Colorado	69.88	Missouri	7.46
California	106.95	Vermont	89.65	South Dakota	69.00	Nebraska	69.06	Tennessee	7.31
New Hampshire	105.61	Pennsylvania	89.39	Massachusetts	68.23	North Dakota	69.00	Georgia	7.02
Indiana	104.09	Kentucky	89.03	Vermont	68.03	New Mexico	67.39	Virginia	6.99
Vermont	103.84	Montana	88.77	Wyoming	66.63	Georgia	66.75	Idaho	6.94
Utah	103.80	Utah	88.04	Ohio	66.61	South Dakota	66.33	Ohio	6.77
Colorado	103.02	West Virginia	87.88	New York	66.43	Alaska	66.31	Wisconsin	6.44
West Virginia	102.81	Iowa	87.26	West Virginia	65.68	Arkansas	66.14	North Dakota	6.32
Washington	101.60	Virginia	87.22	North Carolina	65.26	Montana	65.94	Iowa	6.24
Wisconsin	101.38	Colorado	86.46	Texas	64.83	New Hampshire	65.19	Michigan	6.18
Minnesota	101.37	New Hampshire	86.43	Maryland	64.70	Texas	65.07	Arizona	6.03
Alaska	101.28	Minnesota	86.02	Washington	64.66	Guam	64.81	Kentucky	5.99
Maine	100.53	Idaho	85.92	New Jersey	64.64	Indiana	64.69	Hawaii	5.95
New Jersey	99.92	Missouri	85.91	Guam	63.39	North Carolina	64.53	Pennsylvania	5.80

Table B-5. (Continued)

State	Paternity Establishment Percentage	State	Cases with Orders Percentage	State	Current Collections Percentage	State	Arrearage Cases Percentage	State	Cost Effectiveness Score
North Carolina	99.74	California	85.81	Colorado	63.32	Utah	64.15	Nebraska	5.78
Hawaii	99.47	Arkansas	85.30	Virginia	62.81	Ohio	64.14	Utah	5.59
Georgia	98.80	Arizona	85.09	Hawaii	62.52	Wisconsin	63.47	North Carolina	5.55
Arkansas	98.11	Wisconsin	84.78	Montana	62.31	Kansas	62.95	New York	5.47
Iowa	97.80	Nebraska	84.63	New Hampshire	62.05	New Jersey	62.37	Florida	5.44
Texas	97.60	Georgia	83.44	Michigan	62.00	Oklahoma	61.64	Oregon	5.41
Puerto Rico	97.39	Massachusetts	83.31	Arkansas	61.58	California	61.58	Indiana	5.35
Pennsylvania	97.32	Maryland	82.90	Georgia	60.79	Maryland	61.57	Wyoming	5.30
Kentucky	95.93	Texas	82.90	Utah	60.03	Washington	61.45	Montana	5.13
New Mexico	94.80	Alabama	82.56	Dist. of Columbia	59.97	Virginia	61.38	Louisiana	5.05
Alabama	94.63	Ohio	82.21	Rhode Island	59.93	Illinois	61.19	West Virginia	4.73
Wyoming	94.50	North Carolina	82.01	Idaho	59.90	West Virginia	61.00	Illinois	4.72
Connecticut	94.47	Nevada	80.96	Delaware	59.79	Florida	60.76	Washington	4.68
Florida	94.37	Kansas	80.43	Oregon	59.70	Mississippi	60.30	New Jersey	4.64
Virginia	93.90	Illinois	80.13	Maine	59.26	Nevada	59.91	Oklahoma	4.58
Kansas	93.46	New York	79.72	Alaska	59.07	Kentucky	59.74	South Carolina	4.56
Missouri	93.46	Puerto Rico	78.51	Indiana	58.88	Massachusetts	59.72	Colorado	4.49
Oregon	93.33	Louisiana	78.14	Illinois	58.62	Connecticut	59.16	Alabama	4.46
Idaho	92.67	Guam	77.28	California	58.56	New York	58.81	New Hampshire	4.31

State	Paternity Establishment Percentage	State	Cases with Orders Percentage	State	Current Collections Percentage	State	Arrearage Cases Percentage	State	Cost Effectiveness Score
Guam	92.65	Indiana	77.27	Kentucky	58.33	Oregon	58.67	Arkansas	4.28
South Carolina	92.50	New Jersey	77.08	Connecticut	58.16	Missouri	58.62	Maryland	4.13
Rhode Island	92.35	Oregon	76.54	Missouri	56.80	Louisiana	58.39	Rhode Island	4.10
Maryland	91.88	Michigan	75.75	Puerto Rico	56.62	Maine	57.85	Alaska	4.00
Michigan	91.52	Florida	75.67	Louisiana	56.22	Tennessee	57.53	Nevada	3.98
Nebraska	91.39	Oklahoma	75.48	Virgin Islands	56.08	Delaware	57.42	Maine	3.84
Massachusetts	91.10	New Mexico	74.98	Kansas	55.37	Idaho	57.20	Connecticut	3.65
Tennessee	90.93	Connecticut	73.70	New Mexico	55.03	Michigan	57.20	Minnesota	3.60
New York	90.55	South Carolina	71.30	Oklahoma	54.90	Rhode Island	56.50	Kansas	3.45
Louisiana	90.50	Tennessee	70.66	Mississippi	54.45	Alabama	56.09	Vermont	3.29
Ohio	90.44	Dist. of Columbia	68.20	Tennessee	53.14	Arizona	54.69	New Mexico	2.71
Mississippi	90.16	Virgin Islands	67.95	Florida	53.06	South Carolina	53.85	Guam	2.31
Dist. of Columbia	90.00	Hawaii	67.81	South Carolina	52.26	Virgin Islands	52.32	California	2.29
Virgin Islands	89.75	Delaware	66.41	Arizona	51.45	Dist. of Columbia	51.89	Delaware	2.23
Illinois	84.95	Rhode Island	65.81	Nevada	51.11	Puerto Rico	50.43	Dist. of Columbia	2.13
Delaware	77.98	Mississippi	58.54	Alabama	50.97	Hawaii	45.37	Virgin Islands	$1.98

Source: Table prepared by the Congressional Research Service based on data from the Office of Child Support Enforcement, Department of Health and Human Services.

Note: The paternity establishment percentage can be greater than 100% because states can take credit for paternities established for children of any age and compare that number established to the number of births outside of marriage for a single year.

End Notes

[1] The 1975 enacting legislation (P.L. 93-647) based incentive payments solely on child support collections made on behalf of welfare (i.e., Aid to Families with Dependent Children (AFDC)) families. In 1984, pursuant to P.L. 98-378, the law expanded the incentive payments formula to include child support collections made on behalf of nonwelfare families. For a legislative history of CSE incentive payments, see **Appendix A**. Also note that the AFDC entitlement program was replaced by the Temporary Assistance for Needy Families (TANF) block grant pursuant to P.L. 104-193 (the 1996 welfare reform law).

[2] P.L. 109-171, effective October 1, 2007, prohibited federal matching of state expenditure of federal CSE incentive payments. However, P.L. 111-5 required HHS to temporarily provide federal matching funds (in FY2009 and FY2010) on CSE incentive payments that states reinvest back into the CSE program. Thus, starting again in FY2011, CSE incentive payments that are received by states and reinvested in the CSE program are no longer eligible for federal reimbursement.

[3] The unaudited incentive performance scores are readily available each year when the federal Office of Child Support Enforcement (OCSE) publishes its preliminary data report. In this report the unaudited scores serve as a proxy for the actual (audited) performance indicator scores upon which actual incentive payments are based. (OCSE does not consistently publish actual (audited) performance indicator scores.)

[4] For additional information on the CSE program, see CRS Report RS22380, *Child Support Enforcement: Program Basics*, by Carmen Solomon-Fears.

[5] A 2011 report found that in aggregate about 16% of the state's share of CSE expenditures is financed with incentive payments. Source: Child Support Enforcement: Departures from Long-term Trends in Sources of Collections and Caseloads Reflect Recent Economic Conditions, U.S. Government Accountability Office, GAO-11-196, January 2011, p. 6.

[6] Under old AFDC law, the rate at which states were reimbursed by the federal government for the costs of cash welfare was the Federal Medical Assistance Percentage (FMAP), which varies inversely with state per capita income (i.e., poor states have a higher federal matching rate, wealthy states have a lower federal matching rate). The FMAP ranges from a minimum of 50% to a statutory maximum of 83%. Like the old AFDC program, current law requires that child support collections made on behalf of welfare (i.e., TANF) families be split between the federal and state governments according to the FMAP. If a state has a 50% FMAP, the federal government is reimbursed $50 for each $100 in child support collections for TANF families; if a state has a 70% FMAP, the federal government is reimbursed $70 for each $100 in child support collections for TANF families. In the first example, the state keeps $50 and in the second example, the state keeps $30. Thus, states with a larger FMAP keep a smaller portion of the child support collections.

[7] The TANF block grant replaced the AFDC entitlement program pursuant to P.L. 104-193, the 1996 welfare reform law. Because the CSE incentive payments have changed significantly since 1975 (when the CSE program was enacted), this report refers to both AFDC families/cases and TANF families/cases, depending on the time frame.

[8] See CRS Report RS22753, *Child Support Enforcement: $25 Annual User Fee*, by Carmen Solomon-Fears.

[9] Under the old incentive payment system, each state received a minimum incentive payment equal to at least 6% of the state's total amount of child support collections made on behalf of AFDC/TANF families for the year, plus at least 6% of the state's total amount of child support collections made on behalf of non-AFDC/TANF families for the year. The amount of a state's incentive payment could reach a maximum of 10% of the AFDC/TANF collections plus 10% of the non-AFDC/TANF collections, depending on the state's ratio of CSE collections to CSE expenditures. There was an additional limit (i.e., cap), however, on the incentive payment for non-AFDC/TANF collections. The incentive payment for such

collections could not exceed 115% of incentive payments for AFDC/TANF collections. In addition, the old incentive payment system incorporated only one performance measure (i.e., cost-effectiveness) in determining incentive payments to states. One of the main criticisms of the old incentive payment system was that it did not provide an incentive for states to improve their programs because every state regardless of performance received the minimum incentive payment. There was general agreement by Congress that states whose CSE programs performed poorly should not be rewarded with federal funds.

[10] The CSE incentive payment system was fully implemented in FY2002.

[11] The incentive payment cap was $504 million in FY2009 and FY2010; $513 million in FY2011; $508 million in FY2012; and is estimated at $530 million for FY2013.

[12] In FY1998, the incentive payment, which at that time came out of the gross federal share of child support collected on behalf of TANF families, was $395 million. Beginning in FY2002, child support incentive payments were no longer paid out of the federal share of child support collections made on behalf of TANF families. Instead, federal funds have been specifically appropriated out of the U.S. Treasury for CSE incentive payments.

[13] Department of Health and Human Services. News Release. *HHS Submits Plan to Congress on New Rewards for States to Improve Child Support Collections.* March 13, 1997.

[14] The CSE program serves both welfare and nonwelfare families in its caseload. OCSE defines a CSE "case" as a noncustodial parent (mother, father, or putative/alleged father) who is now or eventually may be obligated under law for the support of a child or children receiving services under the CSE program. If the noncustodial parent owes support for two children by different women, that would be considered two cases; if both children have the same mother, that would be considered one case.

[15] Go to the following website and scroll nearly to the end of the document to the section entitled How an Incentive Payment is determined: http://www.acf.hhs.gov/programs/css/resource/fy2011-preliminary-report.

[16] At the low end of the performance scale, there is a minimum level below which a state is not rewarded with an incentive payment unless the state demonstrates a substantial improvement over the prior year's performance. Even though substantial improvement is recognized, the law stipulates that the incentive payment in such cases cannot exceed 50% of the maximum incentive possible for that performance measure. The substantial improvement provisions do not apply with respect to the cost- effectiveness performance measure.

[17] It was decided during the negotiations on revising the incentive payment system that, because collecting child support on behalf of TANF and former-TANF families is generally more difficult than collecting child support on behalf of families who had never been on TANF, the incentive formula should provide a greater emphasis on collection in TANF and former TANF cases. Moreover, it was mentioned that collections in TANF cases provide direct savings to the state and federal governments. The incentive payment formula thus doubles the collections made on behalf of TANF and former-TANF cases to give them extra emphasis. (See Office of Child Support Enforcement, Department of Health and Human Services. *Child Support Enforcement Incentive Funding.* Report to the House Ways and Means Committee and the Senate Finance Committee. February 1997. p. 8.)

[18] 45 C.F. R. §305.34. Also see Office of Child Support Enforcement, *Data Reliability Audit Requirements for the Fiscal Year 2011 Reporting Period*, Dear Colleague Letter-DCL-11-15, August 22, 2011.

[19] According to the most recent published data, 51 states/territories passed the data reliability audits for FY2009 (the names of the states/territories that passed and did not pass the audit were not published). Source: U.S. Department of Health and Human Services. Administration for Children and Families, Office of Child Support Enforcement, *Office of Child Support Enforcement FY 2009 Annual Report to Congress.* December 2009— http://www.acf.hhs.gov/programs/css/resource/fy2009-annual-report, p. 12.

[20] According to the federal regulations (45 CFR Part 304.12): Each state calculates the federal government's share of child support payments collected on behalf of TANF families. Then the state retains one-fourth of its annual estimate of incentive payments from the federal government's share of child support collected on behalf of TANF families each quarter. Following the end of a fiscal year, the OCSE will calculate the actual incentive payment the state should have received based on the reports submitted for that fiscal year. If adjustments to the estimate are necessary, the state's quarterly TANF grant award will be reduced or increased because of over- or under-estimates for prior quarters and for other adjustments.

[21] Thereby, the audit of FY2011 (October 1, 2010-September 30, 2011) incentive payment data would usually begin in January 2011 and generally would be completed by July 2011. Once the audit is completed, estimated incentive payments would be reconciled with actual incentive payments.

[22] Title 45 CFR Section 305.1(i) states that " ... data may contain errors as long as they are not of a magnitude that would cause a reasonable person, aware of the errors, to doubt a finding or conclusion based on the data."

[23] *Study of the Implementation of the Performance-Based Incentive System—Interim Report*, by the Lewin Group (Karen Gardiner, Michael Fishman, and Asaph Glosser) and ECONorthwest (John Tapogna). Prepared for the Office of Child Support Enforcement. October 2003. p. 14.

[24] There are three performance measures for which states have to achieve certain levels of performance in order to avoid being penalized for poor performance. These measures are (1) paternity establishment [specifically mentioned in the federal law— Section 409(a)(8)(A) of the Social Security Act], (2) child support order establishment, and (3) current child support collections [these last two performance measures were designated by the HHS Secretary—45 CFR Section 305.40].

[25] The penalty amount is calculated as not less than 2% nor more than 3% of the TANF block grant program for the second year of the deficiency. The penalty amount is calculated as not less than 3% nor more than 5% of the TANF block grant program for the third or subsequent year of the deficiency.

[26] U.S. Department of Health and Human Services, Administration for Children and Families, Office of Child Support Enforcement, *Child Support Enforcement Annual Report to Congress FY2010*, April 12, 2013, p. 12. Note that published data related to penalties usually are in CSE's Annual Report to Congress. The most recent annual report is for FY2010. Although the preliminary data report for FY2011 is available (published), it does not contain data related to audits or penalties.

[27] The OCSE has not yet published actual incentive payment data by state for FY2012.

[28] In FY2002, the states with the highest incentive payments were California, Texas, Pennsylvania, New York, Michigan, Florida, and New Jersey. In FY2011, the states with the highest incentive payments were Texas, California, Florida, New York, Pennsylvania, Ohio, Michigan, and New Jersey. These states also are the most populous states.

[29] The table for the FY2002 data can be found at http://www.acf.dhhs.gov/programs/cse/pubs/2003/reports/prelim_datareport/. The table for the FY2011 data can be found at http://www.acf.hhs.gov/programs/css/resource/fy2011-preliminary-report-table-p- 35.

[30] The median reflects the performance of the middle-ranked state (i.e., the 27th state in rank order), with all states weighted equally.

[31] Although a strategic plan for subsequent and future years has been drafted, the enactment of the Affordable Care Act (P.L. 111-148), technological advances, and resource contraints have resulted in ongoing discussions among interested parties in the CSE program about the future of the program.

[32] As mentioned earlier in the text box, a state may use as its PEP either the CSE PEP or the statewide PEP. The state CSE PEP is based on the entire number of children in the CSE caseload who had been born outside of marriage, regardless of year of birth, and whether paternity had been established for them. If the CSE PEP is more than 100%, then the

number of children on the CSE rolls who were born outside of marriage but had paternity established on their behalf exceeded the number of children on the CSE rolls who were born outside of marriage in any previous year. Whereas, if the statewide PEP is more than 100%, then the number of paternities established in the current fiscal year exceeded the number of babies born outside of marriage in the preceding fiscal year.

[33] According to preliminary FY2002 data, Guam had the maximum PEP score of 452.87, but that score for Guam was excluded because of conflicting data.

[34] U.S. Department of Health and Human Services, Administration for Children and Families, Office of Child Support Enforcement, *Child Support Enforcement Annual Report to Congress FY2010*, April 12, 2013, pp. 11-12.

[35] Goal #3 in the FY2005-FY2009 Strategic Plan of the CSE Program is for all children in the CSE program to have medical coverage.

[36] *Interest on Past-Due Child Support*, http://www.supportguidelines.com/articles/art200301. html.

[37] U.S. Department of Health and Human Services, Administration for Children and Families, Office of Child Support Enforcement, *Child Support Enforcement Annual Report to Congress FY2010*, April 12, 2013, p. 12.

[38] OCSE has not yet published data showing the incentive payments received by states in FY2012.

[39] Pursuant to §458(b)(5)(C) of the Social Security Act, a state's collections base = 2 x (TANF collections + Formerly on TANF collections) + Never on TANF collections + Fees retained by other states.

[40] Texas was ranked second highest with regard to incentive payments in FY2002 and FY2005 and highest in FY2010 and FY2011.

[41] California collected 31% more in child support payments than Texas in FY2002 and 25% more in child support payments than Texas in FY2005. Texas collected 32% more in child support payments than California in FY2010 and 44% more in FY2011. Given that the incentive formula gives more weight to child support collections made on behalf of TANF and former-TANF families than on families that have never been on TANF, it is important to note that the majority of the child support collected in California for the four years displayed was on behalf of TANF and former-TANF families. Specifically, in FY2002, FY2005, FY2010, and FY2011, 75%, 65%, 63%, and 63% (respectively) of CSE collections in California were made on behalf of TANF and former-TANF families. The comparable figures for Texas are: 59%, 59%, 54%, and 54%.

[42] One jurisdiction, the Virgin Islands, received incentive payments in four rather than five performance areas. The Virgin Islands failed to meet the cost-effectiveness threshold.

[43] P.L. 104-193 (enacted August 22, 1996), the 1996 welfare reform law directed the HHS Secretary to develop a new revenue- neutral performance-based incentive payment system in consultation with state CSE directors. The federal Office of Child Support Enforcement (OCSE) convened an Incentive Funding Work Group in late 1996 to develop a new incentive payment system. The work group consisted of 26 persons representing state and local CSE programs, HHS regional offices, and the OCSE central office. The work group determined the minimum and maximum standards (i.e., thresholds) for each performance measure based on historic performance by the states and state trends. In general, the upper threshold was based on the view that most states could realistically achieve that level of performance.

[44] States are able to establish paternities for more than 100% of children needing paternity established because the paternity establishment performance measure compares current year data to previous year's data and includes paternity established on behalf of newborns born outside of marriage as well as older children who were born outside of marriage.

[45] States that fail to attain an applicable percentage score of 40% with respect to arrearage collections can still earn an incentive payment if the state improves its performance by at least 5 percentage points over its previous year's score. A financial penalty is not imposed

on states that fail to meet specified performance levels with respect to the arrearage collections performance measure.

[46] Office of Child Support Enforcement, *Report on State Child Support Enforcement Performance Penalties: Recommendations of the State/Federal Penalties Work Group*, July 27, 1998. See also: *Study of the Implementation of the Performance-Based Incentive System—Final Report*, by the Lewin Group (Karen Gardiner, Michael Fishman, and Asaph Glosser) and ECONorthwest (John Tapogna), Prepared for the Office of Child Support Enforcement, 2004. See also: U.S. Government Accountability Office, *Child Support Enforcement: Departures from Long-term Trends in Sources of Collections and Caseloads Reflect Recent Economic Conditions*, GAO-11-196, January 2011.

[47] *Report on State Child Support Enforcement Performance Penalties: Recommendations of the State/Federal Penalties Work Group*, July 27, 1998, p. 7.

[48] *Study of the Implementation of the Performance-Based Incentive System—Final Report*. Prepared for the Office of Child Support Enforcement by the Lewin Group (Karen N. Gardiner, Michael E. Fishman, and Asaph Glosser) and ECONorthwest (John Tapogna), 2004, pp. 18-19.

[49] U.S. Department of Health and Human Services, Administration for Children and Families, Office of Child Support Enforcement, *21 Million Children's Health: Our Shared Responsibility*, The Medical Child Support Working Group, June 2000.

[50] At the March 2-3, 1999 meeting, the Medical Child Support Working Group reviewed available data on medical support. Only seven states were able to provide data and some of those states had concerns about its validity. Census data was also reviewed and found to be unsatisfactory because it included information beyond the CSE program's caseload and the data could not be segregated by state. The Working Group agreed that a performance standard for medical support enforcement could not be set based on such limited and invalid data. (Source: U.S. Department of Health and Human Services, Report to the Congress on Development of a Medical Support Incentive for the Child Support Enforcement Program, June 23, 1999.)

[51] Under current federal law, states are accountable for providing reliable data on a timely basis or they receive no incentive payments. The data reliability provisions were enacted as part of P.L. 105-200, which established the current incentive payment system. They are in the law to ensure the integrity of the incentive payment system. The federal Office of Child Support Enforcement (OCSE) Office of Audit performs data reliability audits to evaluate the completeness, accuracy, security, and reliability of data reported and produced by state reporting systems. The audits help ensure that incentives under the Child Support Performance and Incentives Act of 1998 (P.L. 105-200) are earned and paid only on the basis of verifiable data and that the incentive payments system is fair and equitable. If an audit determines that a state's data are not complete and reliable for a given performance measure, the state receives zero payments for that measure. If states do not meet the data quality standards, they do not receive incentive payments and are subject to federal financial penalties.

[52] Office of Child Support Enforcement, Action Transmittal, AT-11-10, *Notice of Changes to the OCSE-157 Form Regarding Medical Support*, October 17, 2011.

[53] Before FY2008, the federal government was required to match (at a 66% rate) incentive funds that states reinvested in the CSE program. P.L. 109-171 prohibited federal matching of incentive payments effective October 1, 2007 (i.e., FY2008). P.L. 111-5 temporarily reinstated federal matching of incentive payments for FY2009 and FY2010. There is currently no federal match on incentive payments.

[54] The previous 66% federal matching rate on incentive payments resulted in a near tripling of state CSE funding—in that for every dollar the state reinvested in the CSE program, the federal government matched that investment with about $2. Thereby, under old law, states were able to significantly leverage their investment through the federal financial structure.

[55] More additional information on medical child support, see CRS Report R43020, *Medical Child Support: Background and Current Policy*, by Carmen Solomon-Fears.

[56] The Effects of Child Support on Welfare Exits and Re-entries, by Chien-Chung Huang, James Kunz, and Irwin Garfinkel. *Journal of Policy Analysis and Management, Vol. 21, No. 4*, p. 557-576 (2002); http://www.lafollette.wisc.edu/Courses/PA882/Huangm%20et%20al_JPAM.pdf.

[57] Urban Institute, prepared for the Department of Health and Human Services, Administration for Children and Families, Office of Child Support Enforcement, *Child Support Cost Avoidance in 1999, Final Report*, by Laura Wheaton, June 6, 2003, Contract No. 105-00-8303; http://www.acf.dhhs.gov/programs/cse/pubs/2003/reports/cost_avoidance/#N10026.

[58] National Conference of State Legislatures. *Issue Brief: Accurately Evaluating State Child Support Program Performance*, by Teresa A. Myers; http://www.ncsl.org/programs/cyf/PerformIB.htm.

[59] *Federal Register, Vol. 64, No. 249*. Office of Child Support Enforcement, Department of Health and Human Services. Child Support Enforcement Program; Incentive Payments, Audit Penalties. Final Rule. December 27, 2000 (p. 50 of 71).

[60] Even in cases in which the amount of the child support payment incentive is larger than the amount of the TANF penalty imposed, a state is required to reinvest its incentive payment in its CSE program, while penalties are assessed from the TANF funding stream. States that acquire a penalty would find that each quarterly TANF payment for the upcoming year would be reduced for a total of the TANF penalty amount. These states would then additionally have to expend an equivalent amount of state funds if they wanted to replace the reduction of federal funds.

[61] Under this alternative improvement formula, the CSE incentive payment can never be more than half (50%) of the maximum incentive possible. The cost-effectiveness performance indicator is the only measure whereby improved performance does not translate into an incentive payment.

[62] The percentage reduction depends on number of times a state fails to comply with CSE state plan requirements (i.e., at least 1% but not more than 2% for the 1st failure to comply, at least 2% but not more than 3% for the 2nd failure, and at least 3% but not more than 5% for the 3rd and subsequent failures).

[63] The original Paternity Establishment Percentage (PEP) was enacted into law as part of the Family Support Act of 1988 (P.L. 100-485, Section 452(g) of the Social Security Act). The Omnibus Budget Reconciliation Act of 1993 (P.L. 103-66) increased the percentage of children for whom a state must establish paternity (PEP) from 50% to 75%. P.L. 103-66 also imposed financial penalties against states that failed to comply with the mandatory paternity standards. The financial penalty translated into a reduction in federal matching funds for the state's AFDC program. P.L. 104-193, the 1996 welfare reform law, raised the PEP from 75% to 90%.

[64] A state with a paternity establishment percentage at a level between 75% and 90% is required to increase its paternity establishment percentage by two percentage points over the previous year's percentage. A state with a paternity establishment percentage at a level between 50% and 75% is required to increase its paternity establishment percentage by three percentage points over the previous year's percentage. A state with a paternity establishment percentage at a level between 45% and 50% is required to increase its paternity establishment percentage by four percentage points over the previous year's percentage. A state with a paternity establishment percentage at a level between 40% and 45% is required to increase its paternity establishment percentage by five percentage points over the previous year's percentage. A state with a paternity establishment percentage at a level less than 40% is required to increase its paternity establishment percentage by six percentage points over the previous year's percentage.

[65] *Incentive Funding Work Group: Report to the Secretary of Health and Human Services.* January 31, 1997. p. 9.

[66] National Council of Child Support Directors. Position Paper on *Paternity Performance Penalty Revisions*, February 24, 2005.

[67] Ibid.

[68] As noted earlier, P.L. 105-200 stipulated that the aggregate incentive payment to the states could not exceed the following amounts, i.e., $422 million for FY2000, $429 million for FY2001; $450 million for FY2002; $461 million for FY2003; $454 million for FY2004; $446 million for FY2005; $458 million for FY2006; $471 million for FY2007; and $483 million for FY2008. For years after FY2008, the aggregate incentive payment to the states is to be increased to account for inflation. In FY2009, the incentive payment cap was $504 million. It was also $504 million in FY2010, and it was $513 million in FY2011.

[69] *Study of the Implementation of the Performance-Based Incentive System—Final Report*, by the Lewin Group (Karen Gardiner, Michael Fishman, and Asaph Glosser) and ECONorthwest (John Tapogna), Prepared for the Office of Child Support Enforcement, 2004, p. 23. See also: National Child Support Enforcement Association, Resolution on the Incentive Cap, Adopted by NCSEA Board of Directors on August 11, 2001.

[70] A 2003 study and a 2007 study by the Lewin Group indicated that for the nation as a whole, federal CSE incentive payments represented about 25% of CSE financing for the states. In other words, CSE incentive payments represented about 25% of all funds used to draw down the federal match for the CSE program. (Source: The Lewin Group, *Anticipated Effects of the Deficit Reduction Act Provisions on Child Support Program Financing and Performance Summary of Data Analysis and IV-D Director Calls*, Prepared for the National Council of Child Support Directors by the Lewin Group and ECONorthwest, July 20, 2007, p. 4..

Also see U.S. Department of Health and Human Services, *State Financing of Child Support Enforcement Programs: Final Report*, prepared for the Assistant Secretary for Planning and Evaluation and the Office of Child Support Enforcement, prepared by Michael E. Fishman, Kristin Dybdal of the Lewin Group, Inc. and John Tapogna of ECONorthwest, September 3, 2003, p. iii.)

[71] The general CSE federal matching rate is 66%. This means that for every dollar that a state spends on its CSE program, the federal government will reimburse the state 66 cents. So if the state spends $1 on its program, the federal share of that expenditure is 66 cents and the state share of that expenditure is 34 cents. The algebraic formula for this relationship is represented by $.66/.34=x/1$. Thereby, if the state share of the expenditure is $1, the federal share is $1.94 (i.e., the federal share is 1.94 times the state share), and the total expenditure by the state is $2.94 ($1+$1.94). Similarly, if the state share of expenditures amounted solely to the incentive payment of $471 million (i.e., the statutory cap on the aggregate CSE incentive payment for FY2007), the federal share would amount to 1.94 times that amount, or $914 million, translating into $1.385 billion in total CSE expenditures/funding.

[72] Thus under prior law, the incentive payments to the state could be leveraged by about $3 for every $1 expended. This example is based on incentive payment spending (on CSE activities) only. The 3:1 leveraging did not apply to all state expenditures, it only applied to state expenditures that were based on the incentive payments that were reinvested back into the CSE program.

[73] Center for Law and Social Policy. *You Get What You Pay For: How Federal and State Investment Decisions Affect Child Support Performance*, by Vicki Turetsky. December 1998. See also National Conference of State Legislatures. *Issue Brief: Accurately Evaluating State Child Support Program Performance*, by Teresa A. Myers. http://www.ncsl.org/programs/cyf/ PerformIB.htm

[74] U.S. Department of Health and Human Services, Administration for Children and Families, Office of Child Support Enforcement, *Child Support Enforcement Anual Report to Congress FY2010*, April 12, 2013, p. 12.

[75] U.S. Department of Health and Human Services. Administration for Children and Families. *Fiscal Year 2008—Justification of Estimates for Appropriations Committees. Child Support Enforcement.* p. 443-445.

[76] U.S. Government Accountability Office, *Child Support Enforcement: Departures from Long-term Trends in Sources of Collections and Caseloads Reflect Recent Economic Conditions,* GAO-11-196, January 2011, pp. 20-21.

[77] According to the Congressional Budget Office cost estimate of the Deficit Reduction Act of 2005: "If states do not adjust their own spending for the child support program in response to the policies, total funding for the program would fall by 15 percent in 2010. CBO expects that states would instead lessen the effect of the policies on total program spending by increasing state spending. That increased state spending would avoid half of the reduction in total spending that would occur if states were to make no change. CBO estimates that the federal share of administrative costs for child support would fall by about $1.8 billion over the 2008-2010 period and by $5.3 billion over the 2008-2015 period. ... Child support funding is used to establish and enforce child support orders and collect money owed to families. CBO expects that lower spending on the child support program would lead to lower collections." (Source: Congressional Budget Office, Cost Estimate, *S. 1932, Deficit Reduction Act of 2005,* January 27, 2006, p. 59.)

[78] The federal share of AFDC benefit expenditures ranged from 50% to 83%, depending on state per capita income.

[79] U.S. Senate. Committee on Finance. *Social Services Amendments of 1974; a report to accompany H.R. 17045.* December 14, 1974. S.Rept. 93-1356. p. 50-51.

[80] The CSE program was enacted as Title IV-D of the Social Security Act.

[81] P.L. 93-647 stipulated that child support payments on behalf of AFDC families were to be paid to the states following an assignment of child support rights by the AFDC client to the state. Because federal dollars were used to finance a portion of the state AFDC benefit payment, states were required to split child support payments collected on behalf of AFDC families with the federal government. The child support collections obtained on behalf of AFDC families are divided between the state and the federal government according to their respective share of total AFDC benefit payments (a small percentage of AFDC collections is paid directly to families). As noted above, the federal share of AFDC benefit expenditures ranged from 50% to 83%, depending on state per capita income. The federal share is also called the Federal Medical Assistance Percentage or FMAP.

[82] Before 1984, a state that initiated a successful action to collect child support from another state did not receive an incentive payment. Rather, the state that made the collection received the incentive payment. P.L. 98-378 stipulated that each state involved in an interstate child support collection be credited with the collection for purposes of computing the incentive payment. This "double-counting" was intended to encourage states to pursue interstate child support cases as energetically as they pursued intrastate child support cases.

[83] The total amount of incentives awarded for non-AFDC collections could not exceed the amount of the state's incentive payments for AFDC collections for FY1986 and FY1987. The incentive paid for non-AFDC collections was capped at 105% of the incentive for AFDC collections for FY1988, 110% for FY1989, and 115% for FY1990 and years thereafter.

[84] The incentive payment system had been criticized for focusing on only one aspect of the CSE program: cost-effectiveness. It was faulted for not rewarding states for other important aspects of child support enforcement, such as paternity and support order establishment. In addition, because all states received the minimum incentive payment amount of 6% of both AFDC and non- AFDC collections regardless of the state's performance, many analysts claimed that the CSE incentive payment system did not have a real incentive effect.

[85] U.S. Department of Health and Human Services. Administration for Children and Families. Office of Child Support Enforcement. *Child Support Enforcement Incentive Funding.*

Report to the House of Representatives Committee on Ways and Means and the Senate Committee on Finance. February 1997.

[86] Before FY2002, CSE incentive payments were paid out of the federal share of child support collected on behalf of TANF families. Since October 1, 2001 (when the revised incentive payment system was fully phased-in), CSE incentive payments have been paid with federal funds that have been specifically appropriated out of the U.S. Treasury.

[87] OCSE has not yet published actual CSE incentive payment data by state for FY2012.

In: Child Support Enforcement Program
Editor: Pascal Chollet

ISBN: 978-1-62808-384-2
© 2013 Nova Science Publishers, Inc.

Chapter 4

CHILD SUPPORT ENFORCEMENT: $25 ANNUAL USER FEE[*]

Carmen Solomon-Fears

SUMMARY

P.L. 109-171, the Deficit Reduction Act of 2005, required states to impose a $25 annual user fee for Child Support Enforcement (CSE) services provided to families with no connection to the welfare system. The user fee is to be assessed if the state CSE agency collects at least $500 in child support payments on behalf of the family in a given fiscal year. The law gives the states four options on how to obtain the user fee. According to an August 2012 survey of the 54 jurisdictions with CSE programs, 18 jurisdictions pay the fee with state funds, 4 jurisdictions get the fee from the noncustodial parent, 1 jurisdiction imposes the user fee directly on the custodial parent, and 31 jurisdictions impose the fee indirectly on the custodial parent by retaining the fee from the family's child support payment (after $500 per year has been collected on behalf of the family).

---

[*] This is an edited, reformatted and augmented version of a Congressional Research Service publication, CRS Report for Congress RS22753, prepared for Members and Committees of Congress, from www.crs.gov, dated November 6, 2012.

BACKGROUND

The Child Support Enforcement (CSE) program was enacted in 1975 as a federal-state program (Title IV-D of the Social Security Act) to help strengthen families by securing financial support for children from their noncustodial parent on a consistent and continuing basis and by helping some families to remain self-sufficient and off public assistance by providing the requisite CSE services.

The CSE program provides seven major services on behalf of children: (1) parent location, (2) paternity establishment, (3) establishment of child support orders, (4) review and modification of child support orders, (5) collection of child support payments, (6) distribution of child support payments, and (7) establishment and enforcement of medical child support. Collection methods used by state CSE agencies include income withholding, intercept of federal and state income tax refunds, intercept of unemployment compensation, liens against property, reporting child support obligations to credit bureaus, intercept of lottery winnings, sending insurance settlement information to CSE agencies, authority to withhold or suspend driver's licenses, professional licenses, and recreational and sporting licenses of persons who owe past-due support, and authority to seize assets of debtor parents held by public or private retirement funds and financial institutions.

All 50 states, the District of Columbia, Guam, Puerto Rico, and the Virgin Islands operate CSE programs and are entitled to federal matching funds. The federal government and the states share CSE program costs at the rate of 66% and 34%, respectively. The CSE program serves both welfare and non-welfare families.[1] Families receiving Temporary Assistance to Needy Families (TANF) assistance (Title IV-A), foster care payments (Title IV-E), Medicaid coverage (Title XIX), or food stamp recipients who, at state option, are required by law to cooperate with the CSE agency, automatically qualify for CSE services free of charge. Other families must apply for CSE services, and states must charge an application fee that cannot exceed $25.[2]

ANNUAL CSE USER FEE

P.L. 109-171 (Section 7310), the Deficit Reduction Act of 2005 (enacted February 8, 2006), required families that have never been on the TANF program to pay a $25 annual user fee when the Child Support Enforcement

(CSE) program collects at least $500 in child support annually (from the noncustodial parent) on their behalf.[3]

P.L. 109-171 provides the state with four options on how to collect the fee. The $25 user fee may be (1) retained by the state from child support collected on behalf of the family (but the $25 cannot be part of the first $500 collected in any given federal fiscal year); (2) paid by the custodial parent; (3) recovered/recouped from the noncustodial parent; or (4) paid by the state out of state funds.[4]

The intent of the $25 user fee is to recoup in part the costs of the CSE program to the federal and state governments by decreasing CSE program expenditures.[5] The $25 user fee (from custodial and noncustodial parents) is considered income to the CSE program. The federal and state governments share income to the CSE program (sometimes referred to as cost recovery) at the same rate that they share program costs (i.e., 66% federal and 34% state). The Congressional Budget Office (CBO) estimated that the $25 CSE annual user fee provision would save the federal government $405 million and the state governments $215 million over the nine-year period FY2007-FY2015.[6]

After the $25 user fee was enacted, there was a lot of interest in how it would be implemented. Most of the arguments about the user fee (for and against) concerned the option that permitted states to charge the custodial parent.

Persons in favor of the mandatory $25 annual user fee maintain that it will, to a limited extent, compensate the federal government and the states for operating a CSE program. They claim that even on top of the CSE application fee, the CSE program is still a bargain for custodial parents. They argue that there is no comparison between the nominal fees that the CSE program charges and the much higher fees that a private attorney or collection agency would charge for obtaining child support payments. They say that unlike the CSE application fee, it only applies to those who have received a certain amount of child support payments. They also point out that 72% of custodial parents had income above the poverty level (2009 Census data)[7] and thereby could probably afford to pay the user fee without it negatively affecting their standard of living. In addition, they assert that it is normal practice to charge a fee or user charge for services rendered.

Persons opposed to the mandatory $25 annual user fee (that is imposed on the custodial parent) contend that it treats similarly situated families in an unequal manner. They argue that a low-income custodial parent who has not had to go on welfare needs child support just as much as a custodial parent who formerly was on welfare (i.e., the TANF program). They contend that the

$25 annual fee would impose a new surcharge on working poor families who were previously successful in remaining self-sufficient. They contend that fees generally take away funds that otherwise could be available to the child and the family. They also point out that because the $25 user fee is considered CSE program income, the state gets 34% of the $25 fee ($8.50) and the federal government gets the remaining 66% ($16.50). They claim that the administrative cost of reprogramming a state's automated computer system to account for the fee would outweigh the financial benefit of the fee's increased income to the state. They also say that the financial benefit, if any, to the federal government would be negligible.[8]

According to the Lewin Group/ECONorthwest report entitled *Anticipated Effects of the Deficit Reduction Act Provisions on Child Support Program Financing and Performance Summary of Data Analysis and IV-D Director Calls* (July 20, 2007):

> Many directors noted potential benefits of the fee, including program revenue and instilling a sense of ownership in one's child support case. Directors, though, identified more drawbacks to the fee. All directors expected the cost of programming the statewide automated system would exceed the revenue generated from the fee, at least in the short-term. This occurs at a time when they are already facing budget cuts or foregoing other project enhancements. Some expressed concern that it will take money from low-income families; others fear it will drive customers— largely consistent payers—from the program, hurting not only child support program performance but families as well. One-fourth of the surveyed directors stated that their programs would not charge the fee and would pay the federal share out of program resources.[9]

The final regulation pertaining to the $25 CSE annual user fee includes the following comment from OCSE:

> The Federal Government continues to pay 66 percent of State costs to operate child support enforcement programs. This is a generous matching rate, exceeding the administrative matching rate of other programs such as Medicaid and Food Stamps. Therefore, we do not believe that the annual fee amounts to direct compliance costs on States and local governments, nor does it have a federalism impact.[10]

According to a Government Accountability Office (GAO) report:

Some CSE officials we interviewed stated that their states absorbed the $25 service fee due to concerns that the fee would be a burden, while others said that they charged the fee to custodial parents because their states couldn't afford to absorb the fee due to budgetary constraints. Some of the latter told us that the reason they charged the service fee to custodial, rather than noncustodial, parents was because it was easier administratively. A few also reported that families affected by the fee had voiced little opposition to it.[11]

IMPLEMENTATION OF CSE USER FEE

The provision mandating a $25 annual user fee became effective on October 1, 2006. However, some states had to enact the provision into state law before they could impose the mandatory $25 user fee. The proposed regulations on the user fee were published in January 2007.[12] The final regulations were published on December 9, 2008, and became effective on February 9, 2009.[13]

Table 1 is based on a survey of the states by the National Council of Child Support Directors and information from state CSE agencies. *Table 1* indicates that of the 54 jurisdictions with CSE programs, 18 jurisdictions pay the fee with state funds, 4 jurisdictions get the fee from the noncustodial parent, 1 jurisdiction imposes the user fee directly on the custodial parent, and 31 jurisdictions impose the fee indirectly on the custodial parent by retaining the fee from the family's child support payment (after $500 per year has been collected on behalf of the family).

Table 1. Method By Which $25 CSE Annual User Fee Is Imposed

State	Fee Paid by State Out of State Funds	Fee Paid by Noncustodial Parent	Fee Paid by Custodial Parent	Fee Paid Out of Child Support Payment
Alabama				X
Alaska	X			
Arizona				X
Arkansas		X		
California				X
Colorado				X
Connecticut	X			

Table 1. (Continued)

State	Fee Paid by State Out of State Funds	Fee Paid by Noncustodial Parent	Fee Paid by Custodial Parent	Fee Paid Out of Child Support Payment
Delaware				X
District of Columbia	X			
Florida	X			
Georgia Guam	X			X
Hawaii				X
Idaho				X
Illinois	X			
Indiana		X		
Iowa				X
Kansas	X			
Kentucky				X
Louisiana				X
Maine				X
Maryland[a]	X			
Massachusetts	X			
Michigan				X
Minnesota				X
Mississippi		X		
Missouri		X		
Montana	X			
Nebraska				X
Nevada				X
New Hampshire				X
New Jersey	X			
New Mexico	X			
New York				X
North Carolina				X
North Dakota				X
Ohio		X		
Oklahoma				X
Oregon				X
Pennsylvania[b]	X			
Puerto Rico	X			
Rhode Island	X			

State	Fee Paid by State Out of State Funds	Fee Paid by Noncustodial Parent	Fee Paid by Custodial Parent	Fee Paid Out of Child Support Payment
South Carolina				X
South Dakota	X			
Tennessee				X
Texas				X
Utah				X
Vermont	X			
Virgin Islands	X			X
Virginia				X
Washington				X
West Virginia				X
Wisconsin				
Wyoming				X

Source: Table prepared by the Congressional Research Service on October 11, 2012, based on data from the Office of Child Support Enforcement website (Intergovernmental Reference Guide (IRG)— https://extranet.acf.hhs.gov/irg/welcome.html). The website was last modified on August 10, 2012.

[a] Maryland pays the $25 CSE annual user fee out of state funds for cases in which the annual child support collection is between $500 and $3,499.99. If the annual child support collection is $3,500 or more, the $25 annual CSE user fee is retained from child support payments.

[b] Pennsylvania pays the $25 CSE annual user fee out of state funds for cases in which the annual child support collection is between $500 and $1,999.99. If the annual child support collection is $2,000 or more, the $25 annual CSE user fee is retained from child support payments.

End Notes

[1] In FY2011, of the 15.8 million CSE cases, 13% (2.0 million) were in the TANF program, 43% (6.8 million) had formerly been in the TANF program, and 44% (7.0 million) had never been in the TANF program.

[2] The CSE program enacted in 1975 (P.L. 93-647) at first permitted, and then in 1984 (P.L. 98-378) required, the CSE agency to charge a one-time application fee for families not on welfare. In 1975, the law required that the application fee be reasonable, as determined by federal regulations. In 1984, the law specified that the fee could not exceed $25. The CSE agency may charge this fee to the applicant (i.e., the custodial parent) or the noncustodial parent, or pay the fee out of state funds. In addition, a state may at its option recover costs in excess of the application fee. Such recovery of costs may be either from the custodial parent or the noncustodial parent. Although the application fee is mandatory, federal law allows the state to charge an amount that can range from 1 cent to $25. Many of the states that

charge a $1 or less application fee do so to maximize non-TANF clients' access to CSE services. Many state CSE officials view application fees as a barrier to clients who do not have the financial means to apply for services. They also claim that fees and other charges may discourage clients from seeking services, because the fee is paid regardless of whether any child support is collected on behalf of the family. Others view application fees for non-TANF families as a way to reduce CSE program costs. The legislative history of P.L. 98-378 (S. Rept. 98-387, p. 30-31; April 9, 1984) says: "The Committee believes that this minimal fee requirement represents a reasonable way to help defray some of the costs incurred in processing the application and in providing support enforcement services. This fee would still be significantly less costly to the non-AFDC applicant than the cost of pursuing support enforcement through a private attorney."

[3] Provision of a mandatory $25 annual user fee for non-welfare CSE families has been discussed for many years. Such a proposal was included in the George H. W. Bush Administration's FY1992 budget proposals and in the George W. Bush Administration's FY2003 budget proposals. For additional information, see States' Practices and Perspectives for Assessing Fees for Child Support Services to Applicants not Receiving Aid to Families with Dependent Children, U.S. Department of Health and Human Services, Office of Inspector General, July 8, 1992 http://oig.hhs.gov/oas/ reports/region6/69100048.pdf. Also see Feasibility of Collecting Fees for Child Support Services, by Carol Welch, Washington State, Department of Social and Health Services, Division of Child Support, Fiscal Management, June 2001, http://www1.dshs.wa.gov/pdf/esa/dcs/reports/feestudy.pdf.

[4] If the $25 annual user fee is paid by the state out of state funds, it is not considered an administrative cost of the CSE program and thus is not eligible for 66% federal matching funds.

[5] In FY2011, CSE program expenditures amounted to nearly $5.7 billion; child support payments collected from noncustodial parents by CSE agencies totaled $27.3 billion.

[6] Congressional Budget Office, Cost Estimate of S. 1932 (Deficit Reduction Act of 2005), January 27, 2006, p. 55 and p. 60.

[7] U.S. Census Bureau, Custodial Mothers and Fathers and Their Child Support: 2009, by Timothy S. Grall, P60-240, December 2011, p. 6.

[8] National Child Support Enforcement Association (NCSEA), Resolution on $25 Annual Fee, June 17, 2002, see http://www.ncsea.org/files/Resolution-AnnualFee.pdf.

[9] See http://www.nccsd.net/documents/nccsd_final_report_revised_2_437782.pdf.

[10] Federal Register, vol. 73, no. 237, U.S. Department of Health and Human Services, Office of Child Support Enforcement, Final Rules, December 9, 2008, pp. 74913-74914 (http://www.gpo.gov/fdsys/pkg/FR-2008-12-09/pdf/ E8-28660.pdf#page=1).

[11] U.S. Government Accountability Office, Child Support Enforcement: Departures from Long-term Trends in Sources of Collections and Caseloads Reflect Recent Economic Conditions, GAO-11-196, January 2011, p. 24.

[12] Federal Register, vol. 72, no. 15, January 24, 2007, Child Support Enforcement Program, pp. 3093-3102. The proposed regulations can be found at http://www.acf.dhhs.gov/programs/cse/pol/AT/2007/at-07-01.htm.

[13] Federal Register, vol. 73, no. 237, Department of Health and Human Services, Office of Child Support Enforcement, Final Rules, December 9, 2008, pp. 74898-74921(http://www.gpo.gov/fdsys/pkg/FR-2008-12-09/pdf/E8- 28660.pdf#page=1).

INDEX

Q

R

S

T